The Prayer Ministry
of
The Church

The Prayer Ministry
of
The Church

WATCHMAN NEE

Translated from the Chinese

Christian Fellowship Publishers, Inc.

New York

Available from the Publishers at:
Box 1021
Manassas, Virginia 22110

PRINTED IN U.S.A.

CONTENTS

Being a collection of five messages on prayer
given during the approximate period of
1940–1941.

Scripture quotations are from the
American Standard Version of the Bible
(1901), unless otherwise indicated.

The Prayer Ministry of the Church

And if thy brother sin against thee, go, show him his fault between thee and him alone: if he hear thee, thou hast gained thy brother. But if he hears thee not, take with thee one or two more, that at the mouth of two witnesses or three every word may be established. And if he refuse to hear them, tell it unto the church: and if he refuse to hear the church also, let him be unto thee as the Gentile and the publican. ₍vv. 15–17₎ Verily I say unto you, What things soever ye shall bind on earth shall be bound in heaven; and what things soever ye shall loose on earth shall be loosed in heaven. Again I say unto you, that if two of you shall agree on earth as touching anything that they shall ask, it shall be done for them of my Father who is in heaven. For where two or three are gathered together in my name, there am I in the midst of them. (Matt. 18.15–20)

This Scripture passage can be divided into two parts: verses 15–17 form one part, verses 18–20 form another. By studying both carefully, we may see the relationship between them. Verses 15–17 deal with a specific case, whereas verses 18–20 touch upon a general principle. The particular case cited in verses 15–17 needs to be treated in a special way, and the common principle found in verses 18–20 must be diligently learned. Though the case is mentioned first whereas the principle then follows, nevertheless the words in the second part loom much larger than those in the first part. In other words, the first section is only concerned with an individual situation, whereas the second segment pertains to a general though highly significant principle. The way to deal with the case cited in the first section depends on the principle laid down in the second. The second section is the foundation, while the first section is but the application.

In verses 15–17 the Lord Jesus tells us how to treat a brother who sins against another brother: First go and persuade him. If he does not listen, take one or two witnesses with you and speak to him again. If he still refuses to listen, then tell the church. And if he does not listen to the church, let him be to you as a Gentile and a publican. Now after the Lord Jesus has mentioned the case, He continues by saying: "Verily I say unto you. . . ." What He means by this is that there is a reason why you should act in this way; namely, because there is a tremendous relationship or principle bound up in it all.

Hence we say that verses 18–20 form the basis for verses 15–17.

Here we will not dwell on the particular case described in verses 15–17; we make use of this case merely to introduce ourselves to a great principle. We shall see that we should not only act in this manner to a brother who sins against us but should also react in like manner to tens of thousands of other situations. Let us now come to the second part of this passage before us and notice what God intends to show us in particular.

The Earth Governs Heaven

"Verily 1 say unto you, What things soever ye shall bind on earth shall be bound in heaven; and what things soever ye shall loose on earth shall be loosed in heaven." What is characteristic of this verse? The peculiar point here is that the action on earth precedes the action in heaven. Not that heaven binds first, but that the earth binds first; not that heaven looses first, but that the earth looses first. Since the earth has already bound it, heaven will also bind it; since the earth has loosed it, heaven will also loose it. The action of heaven is governed by the action on earth. All that contradicts God needs to be bound, and all that agrees with God needs to be loosed. Whatever the thing may be, whether it should be bound or loosed, such action of binding and loosing begins on earth. The action on earth precedes the action in heaven, for the earth governs heaven.

Let us use some Old Testament examples to illustrate how the earth governs heaven. When Moses on top of the hill held up his hand, Israel prevailed; but when he let down his hand, Amalek prevailed (see Ex. 17.9–11). Who decided the victory or defeat at the foot of the hill? Was it God who willed it or was it Moses? Here we see the principle of God's working, the secret of His action: whatever He wills to do, if man does not will it, He will not do it. We cannot make God do what He does not want to do, but we can hinder Him from doing what He does wish to do. In heaven the issue is decided by God, but before men it is decided by Moses. In heaven God wants the children of Israel to win; yet on earth, if Moses does not hold up his hand Israel will be defeated, but if indeed he holds up his hand Israel will win. The earth governs heaven.

"Thus saith the Lord Jehovah: For this, more-over, will I be inquired of by the house of Israel, to do it for them: I will increase them with men like a flock" (Ez. 36.37). God has a purpose, which is, to increase the number of the house of Israel like a flock. Those who do not know God will say that if He wants to increase the house of Israel like a flock why does He not simply give the increase, for who can stand against Him? But here is the word which God declares—that if He be inquired of concerning this matter by the house of Israel He will do it for them. The principle is unmistakable: God has a purpose already determined, but He will not forthwith do it until He is inquired of by the house of Israel. He wants the earth to govern heaven.

"Thus saith Jehovah, the Holy One of Israel, and his Maker: Ask me of the things that are to come; concerning my sons, and concerning the work of my hands, command ye me" (Is. 45.11). This is a most amazing statement. Are we surprised? Concerning His sons and His work, God says "Command ye me." People dare not utter these three words—"Command ye me"—for how can man ever command God? All who know Him realize that no presumptuous word should ever be uttered before God. Yet He himself offers this word to us: "Concerning my sons and concerning the work of my hands, command ye me." This is none other than earth governing heaven.

Now obviously this in no way can imply that we can force God to do what He will *not* do; not at all. Rather, it simply means that we may command Him to do what He *desires* to do. And this shall be the ground on which we stand. It is because we know God's will that we may say to Him: "God, we want You to do this thing, we are determined that You do it, You cannot but do it." And thus shall we have strong and powerful prayer. How we need to ask God to open our eyes that we may see how His work is done in this dispensation. For during this present age all the works of God are done on this very ground: Heaven desires to do, but heaven will not act right away; it waits for the earth to do first, and then it will do it. Though earth stands second, it nevertheless is also first. Heaven will move only after earth has moved. For God wills to have the earth govern heaven.

Harmonious Will

Someone may be inclined to ask why God should desire the earth to govern heaven? In order to understand such divine desire, we need to remind ourselves that our God is restricted in time. (By time we mean that period between the two eternities. In between eternity past and eternity future there is what we call time.) God is not free to do what He wants. This is the restriction He suffers in having created man. According to the record in Genesis 2, God gave man a free will when He created him. God has His will, but so too has man his will. When a man's will is not in agreement with God's will, God is instantly being restricted. Suppose, for example, that you are all alone in a room containing a table, chairs, a floor and ceiling. You will not be restricted at all by these objects. They simply cannot limit you. Now God is the God of power; He is able to do anything. Had the earth only been filled with things devoid of spirit, God would not be restricted in the least. One day, however, He creates man. This creation is different from a piece of stone or segment of wood; man is not like a table or a chair, incapable of resisting God's ability to place it or move it as He wills. The man whom God has created possesses a free will. He is capable of deciding whether or not he will listen to God, for God has not created a man who *must* hear Him. Upon His having created a man with such a free will, God's power is thereby restricted by this man. He cannot automatically do what He wills to do, but instead He must ask the man whether he himself is also willing. God cannot treat man as though he were wood, stone, a table or a chair—simply because man has a free will. From the day God created man and even up to this present hour, man's free will may either allow or hinder God's authority to get through. For this reason, therefore, we may say that during this period called time which stands between two eternities, the authority of God is restricted by man.

Why should God be restricted in time? Because He knows that in the second eternity—the eternity to come—He will have a harmonious will; that is, man's free will and God's will shall concur. This is the glory of God. An illustration here may be helpful. If you lay a book on a table, it will remain there. Or if you place it on a book shelf, it will stay there too. The book is most obedient to you. Yet you will not be satisfied with such obedience since it is wholly passive because it lacks the element of a free will. In the same manner God takes no pleasure in seeing His created man as passively managed as is a book. Yes, He wants man to obey Him fully, yet He gives man a free will. His desire is to let man exercise his free will to choose to obey. And this is the glory of God!

In the future eternity man's free will shall become one with the eternal will of God. At that time, when

God's eternal purpose is realized, the free will of man comes into perfect harmony with the eternal will of God. In each man's life is a free will, and each free will wills the will of God. In the coming eternity man still has a free will, yet that will stands on God's side. He is able to oppose God, nevertheless he will not oppose Him. Hallelujah! Man indeed possesses the freedom to oppose God; even so, he will not oppose Him. What man does is that which God desires to do. Now such harmonious will as this is truly God's glory!

In the coming eternity man's will is still free; nonetheless his will is in accord with God's. There is no will then that is not subject to God's authority. In time, however, God is restricted by man. What God wants to do, man will not do; if God wants to do much, man will only do little; should God wish to perform greatly, man wishes to perform minutely; or vice versa, as the case might be. How God is not free! In time, God's action is governed by man. By the man here, of course, we mean the church. During the period called time all of God's actions are governed by the church, because the church is to represent the man in the coming eternity. Today the church stands on earth for the will of God. If she is able to meet His will, God will not be restricted. But if she is unable to rise up to that will, God will be restricted. For God wills to do whatever He wants to do through the church. The church today takes in advance the ground which the man of eternity is to take. In the eternity to come, though man's will is still free, he nonetheless stands altogether on the side of God's eternal will. The church today stands on that future ground. Just as God shall be able in eternity to manifest himself through the New Jerusalem—the wife of the Lamb—so He is able now to manifest himself through the body of Christ. Although the church possesses a free will, she puts it in full subjection to the authority of God, as though apart from God's will there is not another free will. Whatever God wants to do, it shall be done. Because the church today places her will completely under God's will, God is able to act as though He is already in the eternity to come since there will not be a second will in the universe to oppose Him. This is the glory of God.

Herein do we see the position on which the church stands before God. Let us not relegate the church to the place where she is viewed as being merely a meeting. No, the church is a group of people who have been redeemed by the precious blood, regenerated by the Holy Spirit, and have meanwhile committed themselves into God's hand, gladly accepting His will, gladly doing His will, and gladly standing on the earth for Him to maintain His testimony.

We need to recognize that God's working today is along a definite line; it is in accordance with a specific law: namely, that for the sake of free will on earth, God refuses to use His own will to overwhelm man. Let us not at all be surprised at this fact. God is in heaven, yet all His movements on earth must first be decided and agreed upon by the will on earth. God will not ignore the will on earth, nor will He take it away and work independently. In all matters related to Him, God will not perform until He obtains the cooperation of the will on earth. Because earth desires it, God will then do it; because the earth so decides, God therefore acts. He must have man's will in harmony with His will. And such a harmony of wills constitutes God's greatest glory indeed!

Three Imposing Principles

We have already mentioned how God has His will concerning all things, but that He will do nothing by himself alone and independently. He will take action only after the free will on earth responds to His will. Were there only the will in heaven, God would make no move; the heavenly move will be accomplished on earth only when He is assured of the same will on earth. This is what we today call the ministry of the church. Believers need to realize that the ministry of the church does not consist merely of the preaching of the gospel—it most certainly does include this, let there be no mistake of that—but also the church's ministry includes the bringing down to the earth the will that is in heaven. But exactly how does the church bring this about? It is by praying on earth. Prayer is not a small, insignificant, non-essential thing as some would tend to think. Prayer is a work. The church says to Him, "God, we want Your will." This is called prayer. After the church knows the will of God, she opens her mouth to ask for it. This is prayer. If the church does not have this ministry, she is not of much use on earth.

Many devotional prayers, prayers of fellowship, and prayers of request cannot be a substitute for prayer as ministry or work. If all our prayers are simply devotional or merely consist of fellowshipping and asking, our prayer is too small. Prayer as work or ministry means that we stand on God's side, desiring what He desires. To pray according to God's will is a most powerful thing. For the church to pray signifies that she has discovered God's will and is now voicing it. Prayer is not only asking God, it is also the making of a declaration. As the church prays, she stands on God's side and declares that what man wants is what He wants. If the church should so declare, the declaration will be at once effectual.

Let us now consider the three imposing principles of prayer to be found in Matthew 18.18–20.

1. Pronouncing the Will of God

"What things soever ye shall bind on earth shall be bound in heaven; and what things soever ye shall loose on earth shall be loosed in heaven" (v.18). Who are the "ye" here? They are the church, because in the preceding verse the Lord mentions the church. So that this is a continuation of verse 17. Therefore, the meaning of this verse 18 now before us is: that whatever things you the church shall bind on earth shall be bound in heaven, and whatever things you the church shall loose on earth shall be loosed in heaven.

Here lies a most important principle: God works through the church today; He cannot do whatever He desires to do unless He does it through the church. This is a most sobering principle. Today God cannot do things by His own Self alone, because there is in existence another free will; without the cooperation of that will God is not able to do anything. The measure of the power of the church today determines the measure of the manifestation of the power of God. For His power is now revealed through the church. God has put himself in the church. If she is able to arrive at a high and great position, the manifestation of the power of God can also arrive at such a high and great position. If the church is unable to reach a high and great position, then God too cannot manifest His power in highness and greatness.

This whole matter can be likened to the flow of water in one's house. Though the water tank of the Water Supply Company is huge, its flow is limited to the diameter of the water pipe in one's house. If a person wishes to have more flow of water, he will need to enlarge his water pipe. Today the degree of the manifestation of God's power is governed by the capacity of the church. Just as at one time earlier, when God manifested himself in Christ, His manifestation was as large as the capacity of Christ; so now, God's manifestation in the church is likewise circumscribed—this time by the capacity of the church. The greater the capacity of the church, the greater the manifestation of God, and the fuller the knowledge of God.

We need to see that in all the things which God does on earth today He will first get the church to stand with Him, and then He will do the work through her. God will not execute anything independently; whatever He does today He does with the cooperation of the church. She is that through which God manifests himself.

Let us repeat that the church is like a water pipe. If the pipe is small it will not be able to convey much water even should the source be as watery as the Yangtze River. God in heaven purposes to do something, but He will not perform it until there is movement on earth. How many are the things which God wants to bind and to loose in heaven! Many are the people and things that are contradictory to Him; and all these God expects to be bound. Many also are those people and things that are spiritual, valuable, profitable, sanctified, and being of God; and these He anticipates to be loosed. But just here a problem arises: Will there be man on earth who will first bind what God wants to bind and loose what He intends to loose? God wills to have the earth govern heaven; He desires His church on earth to govern heaven.

This does not imply that God is not all-mighty, for He is indeed the Almighty God. Yet the all-mightiness of God can only be manifested on earth through a channel. We cannot increase God's power, but we can hinder it. Man is not able to give increase to God's power, nonetheless he can obstruct it. We cannot ask God to do what He does not want to do, yet we can restrict Him from doing that which He does want to do. Do we really see this? The church has a power by which to manage the power of God. She can either permit God to do what He wants or else prohibit Him from doing it.

Our eyes need to foreglimpse the future. One day God will extend His church to be the New Jerusalem, and at that time His glory will be fully manifested through the church without encountering any difficulty. Today God wants the church to loose on earth first before He will loose in heaven; He wants her to bind on earth first before He will bind in heaven. Heaven will not begin to do things. Heaven will only follow earth in its working. God will not start first; He in His operation only follows the church. Oh, if this be the case, what a tremendous responsibility the church has!

As was indicated earlier, what Matthew 18.15–17 refers to is but one individual case; what follows, however, constitutes a great principle. The particular situation is: A brother has sinned against another, yet he will neither acknowledge he has sinned nor confess his fault. When he refuses to listen to the church, he will be looked upon as a Gentile and publican. Now the brother who has sinned will probably retort: Who are you? If you (the church) take me as a Gentile and publican, I will not come again to the meeting. If I cannot come to your meeting, there are still other meetings to which I can go.

But notice here what the Lord Jesus says in return. "Verily, I say unto you, what things soever ye shall bind on earth shall be bound in heaven; and what things soever ye shall loose on earth shall be loosed in heaven." Therefore, when the church judges a person as a Gentile, God in heaven also judges him as a Gentile. When the church looks upon an offending brother as a publican, God in heaven likewise looks upon him as a publican. In other words, what the church does on earth God also will do in heaven.

We have here, then, both a particular case and a governing principle. Our Lord is merely citing the case to prove the general principle. And the principle is: Whatever the church does on earth, God in heaven will do likewise. If the church treats a brother as a Gentile and publican, God in heaven will also treat him as such. This principle is applicable not just in this one case, it is applicable in many other cases. The incident given here serves merely as an example.

The church is God's chosen vessel wherein is placed the will of God so that she may pronounce on earth God's will. If the earth wills, heaven wills too. If the church wills, God also wills. For this reason, what God desires to accomplish in heaven will not be realized on earth if He encounters difficulty in the church.

Many brothers and sisters are bearing heavy

burdens from morning to night. They are so burdened because they do not pray. When a faucet is opened, the water flows; but when it is closed, the water is shut off. Now think for a moment, Which water pressure is greater—that generated in releasing the water or that generated in retaining the water? We all know that when water is released, the pressure is decreased; whereas when it is blocked, the pressure is increased. Even so, when the church prays, it is like opening the water pipe; the longer it is open the more diminished becomes the pressure. By the same token, if the church does not pray, it is like obstructing the water pipe: the pressure will gradually be built up. Whenever God wishes to do a thing He will place a burden upon a brother, a sister, or the whole church. Should the church pray and fulfill her ministry, the more she prays the lighter becomes the burden. Each prayer will lighten a little of her burden. And after ten or twenty times of praying, her inward burden will be greatly lessened. But if the church fails to pray, she shall feel the heavy load and become so suffocated as to imagine herself to be dying.

In view of this, brothers and sisters, whenever you feel heavy and suffocating within, let it be known that it is for no other reason than that you have not fulfilled your ministry before God. Should His burden be upon you, try to pray for half an hour or an hour, and you shall find yourselves breathing more normally once again because the pressure has been greatly decreased.

What, then, is the prayer ministry of the church?

It is God telling the church what He wishes to do so that the church on earth can then pray it out. Such prayer is not asking God to do what *we* want to do, but asking Him to do what *He* wants to do. Oh, let us see that the church is to declare on earth the will of God in heaven. The church is to pronounce on earth that this will of God is what she wants. In case she fails on this point, she will be of very little value in God's hand. Even though she may do well in other matters, she is of little use to God if she is defective in this matter. The highest use of the church to God is to allow His will to be done on earth.

2. Harmony in the Holy Spirit

We have seen how the church ought to bind what God wishes to bind and to loose what God wishes to loose. How, though, is the church actually to bind and to loose? "Again I say unto you, that if two of you shall agree on earth as touching anything that they shall ask, it shall be done for them of my Father who is in heaven" (verse 19). The preceding verse, verse 18, lays stress upon both the earth and heaven, but so does this verse. Verse 18 speaks of heaven binding or loosing whatever the earth binds or looses, but so too does verse 19, which says that the heavenly Father will do whatever the earth asks for. Please note that what the Lord Jesus emphasizes here is not simply an agreeing in the asking of any one thing, rather is it an agreeing on earth as touching *every*-thing whatever they shall ask. He does not mean to say that two persons agree on earth touching a certain thing and they then ask for it; no, the Lord Jesus is saying that if you agree on *every*thing,* then whatever *particular* point you shall ask for, it shall be done for them of His Father who is in heaven. This is the oneness of the body, or may it be said, the oneness in the Holy Spirit.

If a person's flesh has not been dealt with, he will consider himself a superman since, in his view, heaven must hear him. No, if you are not in the oneness of the Holy Spirit, nor are praying in the harmony of the Holy Spirit, just see whether heaven will hear you at all. You may pray, but heaven will not bind what you bind nor loose what you loose. For this is not something you are capable of doing by yourself. If you think you *can* do it alone, you plainly think foolishly. For what the Lord declares is this: "If two of you shall agree on earth as touching anything that they shall ask, it shall be done for them of my Father who is in heaven." This means should two of you be harmonious concerning any and every matter —being just as harmonious as is music—then whatever item you shall ask for, it shall be done for you by the heavenly Father. To pray such prayer requires the work of the Holy Spirit in the persons who pray. That is to say, I as one brother am brought by God to a place where I deny all my desires and will only what the Lord wants and another brother is likewise brought by the Holy Spirit to that place of denying all his desires and wanting only what the Lord wills. I

---

* The meaning here is not the *literal* concurrence on everything between two persons, but the harmony in the Holy Spirit as described by the author in the paragraphs that follow.—*Translator*

and he, he and I, are both brought to a place where there is such harmony as is true in music. And then, whatever we shall ask, God in heaven will perform for us.

Brethren, do not fancy that simply so long as we concur on an item for prayer (without a prior harmony in the Holy Spirit), our prayer will be heard. Not so. People with the same idea often have many conflicts. Merely having the same aim does not guarantee the absence of discord. Two may both want to preach the gospel, but they may still quarrel between themselves. Two may completely desire to help others, nevertheless they rub against one another. Sameness in purpose does not necessarily mean harmony. We ought to realize that there is no possibility of harmony in the flesh. Only when our natural life is dealt with by the Lord and we begin to live in the Holy Spirit—I living in Christ as well as you living in Christ—will we ever have harmony, and will we ever then be able to pray with one accord on a given matter.

Here then are two facets of one thing: the first is a being in harmony about everything, the second is a praying for anything. We need to be brought by God to such a place as this. Apart from the body of Christ there is no place where Christian harmony may be found. Harmony is in the body of Christ. Only there is there the absence of strife, only there is there harmony. If our natural life is dealt with by the Lord and we are brought to really know what the body of Christ is, then are we in harmony and our prayer together will be in harmony too. Because we stand on the ground of harmony, we also agree on any particular matter. Since what we see is harmonious, we are qualified to be the mouthpiece of God's will. Brothers and sisters, when you are praying for a certain matter, if you have a different opinion be careful lest you err. Only when the whole church gathers together and agrees on that matter do we find that heaven wills to do it. For this reason, therefore, let us trust the church.

Keep in mind that prayer is not the first thing to be done. Prayer only follows on the heels of harmony. If the church desires to have such a ministry of prayer on earth, each and every brother and sister must learn to deny the life of the flesh before the Lord, else the church will not be effective. The word which the Lord Jesus gives us here is most wonderful. He does not say that if you ask in His name the Father will hear you; nor does the Lord say that He will pray for them that the Father may answer. Instead, He declares: "If two of you shall agree on earth as touching anything that they shall ask, it shall be done for them of my Father who is in heaven." Oh! If we really agree, the gate of heaven shall be opened!

Here is a brother who sins against another brother. Before the church begins to deal with him, that brother who is being sinned against goes with another brother or two to persuade him unto repentance. These two brothers go to that brother who has sinned before the church ever begins to deal with him. Yet, not that these two brothers see differently from the church; only, they see it in advance of the church, for subsequently the church sees the situation exactly the same way. In other words, these two brothers stand on the ground of the church. What the Lord means is that the two of them on earth represent the church on earth. What the church sees is in perfect agreement with what these two brothers see. This is the ministry of prayer. They must agree on everything whatsoever it may be, and they must pray with one accord on that particular thing.

The prayer ministry of the church is a praying on earth so as to cause action in heaven. We should remember that prayer such as is given in Matthew 18 is definitely not included in devotional prayer or in private personal prayer. Many times we have personal needs for which we ask God and He answers us. There is indeed a place for personal prayer. Likewise, oftentimes we sense the nearness of God. Thank God, He hears devotional prayers. This too should not be despised. We even acknowledge that should the prayer of a brother or sister go unanswered or should a person not sense the nearness of God, something is wrong. We should pay attention to personal prayer as well as devotional prayer. Especially with young believers, they shall not be able to run the course before them if they are lacking in personal and devotional prayers.

Even so, we need to realize that prayer is not just for personal use, nor is it only for devotional purpose. Prayer is a ministry, prayer is a work. This prayer on earth is the church's ministry as well as her work. It is the responsibility of the church before God, because her prayer is the outlet of heaven. What is the prayer of the church? God desires to do a certain thing, and the church on earth prays for this thing in anticipation so that it may be realized on earth and that God's purpose may be accomplished.

The ministry of the church is the ministry of the body of Christ, and that ministry is prayer. Such prayer is neither for devotional purpose nor for personal need; it is more for "heaven". Now what such prayer as this—in the instance before us here— signifies is as follows: Here is a man who has lost fellowship due to his refusal to listen to the persuasion of one brother, to the advice of two or three other brothers, and finally to the judgment of the church. God will therefore loose a judgment upon him as to be considered a Gentile and a publican; yet God will not act immediately but will wait until the church prays towards that end, and then He will do it in heaven. If the church will take up the responsibility to pray on earth such as this, it will eventually be noticed that this offending man's spiritual life shall begin to dry up as though he has no part with God thereafter. God will undertake to do this, but He awaits the church to pray.

Many matters are piled up in heaven, many transactions remain undone, simply because God is unable to find His outlet on earth. Who knows how very many unfinished matters there are in heaven which God cannot execute because the church has not exercised her free will to stand on His side for the realization of His purpose. Let us understand that the church's noblest work, the greatest task she could ever undertake, is to be the outlet for God's will. For the church to be the outlet of God's will is for her to pray. Such prayer is not fragmentary; it is a prayer ministry—prayer as work. As God gives vision and opens people's eyes to see His will, so people rise up to pray.

The Lord shows us here that individual prayer is inadequate; it takes at least two to pray. If we do not see this, we will not be able to know what the Lord is talking about. The prayers in the Gospel according to John are all personal. Hence we find such a word as: "Whatsoever ye shall ask of the Father in my name, he may give it you" (15.16). There is no condition laid down as to the number of persons. In Matthew 18, however, a numerical condition is given; namely, at least two. "If two of you . . . on earth . . .", says the Lord. There needs to be at least two because in this passage we have the matter of fellowship. It is not something done by one person, nor is it one person who serves as God's outlet, but it is two.

The principle of two persons is the principle of the church, which is also the principle of the body of Christ. Though such prayer is prayed by two persons, to "agree" is indispensable. To agree is to be harmonious. Those two individuals must be harmonious, must stand on the ground of the body, and must know what the life of the body is. These two here have but one aim, which is to say to God: We want Your will to be done—as in heaven, so on earth.

When the church stands on such a ground and prays accordingly, we will see that whatever is prayed shall be done by the heavenly Father.

When we truly stand on the ground of the church and take up this responsibility of prayer ministry before God, the will of God shall be done in the church where we are. Otherwise, the church in one's locality is vain. Such prayer, whether prayed by few or by many, must be a strong prayer. For the degree of God's working today is governed by the degree of the prayer of the church. The manifestation of God's power may not exceed the prayer of the church. Today the greatness of God's power is circumscribed by the greatness of the church's prayer. This does not mean, of course, that the power of God in heaven is only that great and no more, for obviously in heaven His power is unlimited. Only on earth today is the manifestation of His power dependent on how much the church prays. Only by the prayer of the church can the manifested power of God be measured.

In view of this, the church should pray big prayers and make big requests. How can the church pray small prayers when she comes before the God of such abundance? She cannot make little requests before such a great God. To come before the great God is to expect great things to happen. If the capacity of the church is limited, it cannot help but restrict the manifestation of God's power. Let it be recognized that the matter of the overcomers has not yet been fully solved nor has Satan been cast into the bottomless pit. For the sake of His testimony, therefore, God must obtain a vessel through which He may do all His works. It needs the church to pray tremendous prayers in order to manifest God. And this is the ministry of the church.

Brothers and sisters, we wonder whether God, in visiting our prayer meeting, can confirm that it truly fulfills the prayer ministry of the church. We must see that it is not a question of the number of times, rather is it a matter of whether there is weight. If we really see the prayer responsibility of the church, we cannot but confess how inadequate is our prayer, how we have restricted God and hindered Him from doing all He wants to do. The church has failed in her ministry! How mournful is this situation!

Whether or not God is able to have a church which is faithful to her ministry depends on whether a group of people disqualify themselves before God or become true vessels of His in the realization of His purpose. We want to shout forth that what God looks for is the faithfulness of the church to her ministry. The ministry of the church is prayer—not the ordinary kind consisting of small prayers but the kind which prepares the way of God. It is God who first desires to do a certain thing, but the church prepares the way for it with prayer so that He may have a thoroughfare. The church should have big prayers, terrific and strong prayers. Prayer is not a light matter before God. If prayer is always centered upon self, upon personal problems and upon small gain or loss, where can there be the way for the eternal purpose of God to get through? We need to be pushed to the depth in this matter of prayer.

For "two to agree" is not a superficial word or light expression. If we do not know what the body of Christ is, nor stand on such a ground, we will be ineffective though we may gather two hundred people to pray. But if we in fact see the body of Christ and stand in the rightful place in the body—denying our flesh and not asking for ourselves but for the will of God to be done on earth—we shall see how harmonious is such prayer. In this way, that for which we pray on earth shall be done for us by the Father who is in heaven.

Please notice that verse 18 includes those very precious words, "what things soever", and verse 19 too has an equally precious word: "anything". "What things soever ye shall bind on earth shall be bound in heaven; and what things soever ye shall loose on earth shall be loosed in heaven." The Lord signifies that as much as the earth binds, the heaven also binds; and that as much as the earth looses the heaven also looses. The measure of the earth decides the measure in heaven. There need be no fear of having too large a measure on earth, because the measure in heaven is always intrinsically greater than that of the earth and that therefore no chance exists for the measure on earth to overtake that of heaven. What heaven wishes to bind is invariably far more than what the earth wishes to bind; and what heaven wishes to loose always exceeds what the earth will loose. Such binding and loosing is beyond any single person. It can only be done "if two . . . shall agree on earth as touching anything that they shall ask," and then "it shall be done for them of my Father who is in heaven."

Brethren, the power of God is forever greater than our power. The water in the water tank of the company unquestionably has more volume than the water in our pipes. The water in the well is always more abundant than the water in our bucket. The power of heaven can never be measured by earthly eyesight.

3. Are Gathered Together

"For where two or three are gathered together in my name, there am I in the midst of them" (v.20). Here is the third principle, and the most profound of them too. In verse 18 we have a principle, in verse 19 another principle, and verse 20 still another. The principle given in verse 20 is broader than that of verse 19. Why does verse 19 say that "if two of you shall agree on earth as touching anything that they shall ask, it shall be done for them of my Father who is in heaven"? The answer is given in verse 20: "For where two or three are gathered together in my name, there am I in the midst of them." Why is there such great power on earth? Why does praying in harmony have such tremendous effect? What gives the praying in harmony of two or three persons this much power? It is because whenever we are called to gather together in the name of the Lord the presence of the Lord himself is there. This is the cause of agreement. Verse 18 speaks of the relation between earth and heaven; verse 19, of the prayer of harmony on earth; verse 20, of the cause for such harmony.

Let us realize that we are *called* to gather. We do not gather by ourselves; we are called to gather together. To gather by ourselves and to be called to gather are two vastly different things. To be called to gather is to be called by the Lord to gather together. We do not come by ourselves; rather, the Lord has called us. Many come to a meeting in the attitude of observing or attending, and consequently they get nothing. If anyone comes because the Lord has spoken to him, that one will have a sense of loss if he does not come. People who are thus called by the Lord to gather are gathered together in the name of the Lord. They come for the sake of the Lord's name. Such brothers and sisters can say wherever they come together: "We are here not for ourselves, but for the Lord's name, for the sake of glorifying Your Son."

Thank God, when all the brothers and sisters are gathered together in the name of the Lord there is agreement, there is harmony. In the event we come to a meeting for our own sake, there will obviously not be any harmony. But if we will have what the Lord wills and not what we will, and if we will reject what the Lord rejects and not what we reject, then there will be agreement. Hence the children of God are being called by the Lord to gather together. They are gathered in His name. Says the Lord, "There am I in the midst of them." It is the Lord who is directing everything. Since He is here directing, enlightening, speaking and revealing, therefore what things soever shall be bound on earth shall also be bound in heaven and what things soever shall be loosed on earth shall be loosed in heaven. It is all because the Lord is here working together with His church.

We consequently need to learn how to deny ourselves before the Lord. Each time He calls us to gather together we should be turned to His name, for His name is higher than all other names. All idols must be smashed. Thus shall He lead us.

Brothers and sisters, this is not feeling nor theory, but fact. If the church is normal, then after each gathering she knows whether the Lord is here. When the Lord is present, the church is rich and strong. During such time she can either bind or loose. But if the Lord is not in the midst, she can do nothing. Only the church possesses such power; the individual simply does not have it within him.

May the Lord grant us deeper understanding and experience on prayer. Prayer is not just personal or devotional; it needs to be a work and a ministry. May the Lord sustain us with power so that whenever we gather together we may work with prayer and fulfill the church's ministry in prayer so that the Lord may be able to do all He wants to do.

2 Pray Like This

And when ye pray, ye shall not be as the hypocrites; for they love to stand and pray in the synagogues and in the corners of the streets, that they may be seen of men. Verily I say unto you, They have received their reward. But thou, when thou prayest, enter into thine inner chamber, and having shut thy door, pray to thy Father who is in secret, and thy Father who seeth in secret shall recompense thee. And in praying use not vain repetitions, as the Gentiles do; for they think that they shall be heard for their much speaking. Be not therefore like unto them: for your Father knoweth what things ye have need of, before ye ask him. After this manner therefore pray ye: Our Father who art in heaven, hallowed be thy name. Thy kingdom come. Thy will be done, as in heaven, so on earth. Give us this day our daily bread. And forgive us our debts, as we also have forgiven our debtors. And bring us not into temptation, but deliver us from the evil one. For thine is the kingdom, and the power, and the glory, forever. Amen. For if ye forgive men their trespasses, your heavenly Father will also forgive you. But if ye forgive not men their trespasses, neither will your Father forgive your trespasses. (Matt. 6.5–15 margin)

Ordinarily we continually lay stress on having prayer answered. Yet here the Lord Jesus emphasizes having prayer rewarded. How do we know? Because the word "reward" in verse 5 is the same word used in verse 2 regarding alms and verse 16 concerning fast. If reward is prayer answered, then what will it mean in alms and fast? Judging by its context, the reward here refers to the reward obtained at the kingdom time. We are hereby shown that prayer answered is secondary while prayer rewarded is primary. If our prayer is in accordance with the mind of God, it not only will be answered but also be remembered in the future at the judgment seat of Christ for reward. And hence the prayer mentioned here will give us righteousness as well as answer today. In other words, our prayer today is our righteousness.

However, the righteousness of prayer is not obtained by praying carelessly, heartlessly, habitually and improperly. On the contrary, the Lord teaches us here how we should not imitate the prayers of two kinds of people. And He also gives us a model prayer.

Not As the Hypocrites

"And when ye pray," says the Lord, "ye shall not be as the hypocrites: for they love to stand and pray in the synagogues and in the corners of the streets, that they may be seen of men." Prayer is primarily communion with God for the manifestation of God's glory. But these hypocrites use prayer which ought to glorify God to glorify themselves; consequently, they love to pray in the synagogues and in the corners of the streets. They act in this manner in order to be seen of men, since synagogues and street corners are obviously public places where people assemble. They do not pray to be heard of God, they pray instead to be seen of men. They purpose to manifest themselves. Such prayer is exceedingly superficial. It cannot be considered as praying to God nor communion with God. Since the motive of such kind of prayer is to receive glory from men, it has no registration with God, and therefore will not obtain anything from Him. They have received their reward in the praise of men, hence they will not be remembered in the kingdom to come.

How, then, should we pray? The Lord continues: "But thou, when thou prayest, enter into thine inner chamber, and having shut thy door, pray to thy Father who is in secret, and thy Father who seeth in secret shall recompense thee." The phrase "inner chamber" is figurative here. Just as "synagogues" and "street corners" serve to represent exposed places, so "inner chamber" is representative of a hidden place. Brothers and sisters, you may indeed find an inner chamber even on street corners and in synagogues, on thoroughfare as well as in car. Why? Because an inner chamber is that place wherever you commune with God in secret, wherever you do not display your prayer on purpose. "Enter into thine inner chamber, and having shut thy door" means shutting out the world and shutting in yourselves. In other words, we are to disregard all outside voices and to quietly and singly pray to our God.

"Pray to thy Father who is in secret, and thy Father who seeth in secret shall recompense thee." How comforting is this word. Praying to your Father who is in secret requires faith. Although you do not sense anything in the open, you believe you are praying to your Father who is in secret. He *is* in secret, beyond the observation of human eyes, yet He is also really there. He does not despise your prayer, He is there observing. All this is indicative of how much He is attentive to your prayer. He is not only observing, He is even going to recompense you. Can you believe this word?

When the Lord says "shall recompense", He *will* recompense. He is here guaranteeing that your prayer in secret shall not be in vain. If you really pray, He will surely recompense you. Even though there does not seem to be any recompense today, a day *shall* come when you will be rewarded. Brothers and sisters, is your prayer in secret able to stand the scrutiny of your Father who is in secret? Do you believe that the Father who is in secret shall recompense you?

Not As the Gentiles

The Lord not only teaches us not to display ourselves but also instructs us: "In praying use not vain repetitions, as the Gentiles do: for they think that they shall be heard for their much speaking." "Vain repetitions" in the Greek means uttering repetitious monotones in the way a stutterer would speak. In praying, the Gentiles repeat the same word monotonously. Such prayer is mere sound but with no meaning. As you stand nearby to listen to their prayer you will hear a monotonous, repetitive sound as though you were standing by a stream hearing the continuous rippling of water against the rocks or standing by a pebble-filled road and hearing the endless rolling of cart wheels passing over it. The Gentiles intone the same words many times. They think they shall be heard for their much speaking. Yet such prayer is vain and ineffective. We must not pray like that.

For this reason, let not the words of our prayers offered in a prayer meeting be void of meaning. When someone prays and you do not say amen, he will accuse you of not being of one mind. Yet if you do amen his prayer, he will use that word repetitiously. His prayer is not governed by the amount of heart but by the degree of supporting fervor. His prayer is not for the sake of discharging inward burden but to finish a speech. Many are the prayers effected by men, many are the utterances which far exceed the heart. I say again that such prayer is like the sound of rippling water against the rock or of cart wheels rolling endlessly over the pebble road. Such prayer has sound but no meaning. We should not pray like this.

"Be not therefore like unto them: for your Father knoweth what things ye have need of, before ye ask him." This verse shows us that whether or not our prayer is heard by God depends on our attitude before Him as well as our real need. It does not rest upon the much or the less of our words. If what we pray for is not what we need our prayer will go unanswered, however much word we may utter. Asking without need reveals greediness; it is asking amiss. God will gladly supply all our needs, but He is unwilling to gratify our selfish desire. How foolish for some people to say they need not pray since God knows all their needs. For the purpose of prayer is not to notify God but to express our trust, our faith, our expectation, and our heart desire. Hence we should pray. Yet in our praying, the desire of our heart should exceed the word of our lips, and faith should be stronger than word.

"Pray Then Like This"

Now let us see how the Lord teaches us to pray. This prayer is commonly known as the Lord's prayer.

Such a notion is wrong. For this is not the Lord's own prayer; it is the prayer He teaches us to pray. It is most distinctly stated in Luke 11.1–4. We should learn this prayer well.

"After this manner therefore pray ye." To pray like this does not mean to repeat these words each time we pray. No, the Lord does not mean that at all. He is teaching us how to pray, not asking us to repeat these words.

Ever since the world began, prayers have often been offered to God. Generation after generation, time after time, countless people have come to God and prayed. Seldom are there those who pray aright. Many think of what they themselves wish to have, few pay attention to what God wants. For this reason, the Lord Jesus opens His mouth to teach us to pray like this which we see here. And this kind of prayer is possessed of tremendous weight and greatness and depth. Now unless we have no intention to learn, we must learn to "pray like this" if we would learn how to pray at all. For God has come to earth to be a Man, and for the first time this Man tells us that only this kind of prayer is right to the point.

The Lord wants us to pray to "our Father who art in heaven." This name "Father" is a new way for men to address God. Formerly men called Him "the Almighty God", "the Most High God", "the everlasting God", or "Jehovah God"; none dared to call God "Father". Here for the very first time God is addressed as "Father". This plainly indicates that this prayer is offered by those who have been saved and have eternal life. Because men are saved, they can therefore call God "Father". Only those who are begotten of Him are the children of God. They alone can address God as "Father". This is a prayer prayed to "our Father who art in heaven", and hence it is offered up on the ground of being children. How sweet and how comforting to come to God and to declare: "Our Father who art in heaven."

Originally our Lord Jesus alone could call God "Father", but now the Lord wants us also to call Him "our Father". Great indeed is this revelation. Except for the fact that God so loved us and gave His only begotten Son to us, how would we ever be able to call Him "our Father"? Thank God, through the death and resurrection of His Son, we now become the children of God. We have obtained a new position. Hereafter our prayer is prayed to our Father who is in heaven. How intimate, how free, and how exalted! May the Spirit of the Lord give us greater under-standing of God as Father and also the confidence that our Father is both loving and patient. He will not only hear our prayer but cause us to have the joy of prayer as well.

This prayer may be divided into three parts: the first pertains to the things of God—being the prayer of our three heart desires towards God (vv.9,10) and most basic in nature; the second pertains to our own affairs—being our requests for God to protect us (vv.11–13a); while the third is our declaration—being our praises to God (v.13b). Let us now consider each of them separately.

Three Heart Desires towards God

The initial section pertains to the three heart desires towards God.

The very first desire is "Hallowed be thy name". God has an expectation today, which is, that we pray that His name may be honored. His name is highly exalted among the angels, yet His name is abused carelessly by men. When His name is taken in vain by men He does not express His wrath by thundering from heaven. He instead hides himself as though non-existent. He has never done anything against men for His name to be used in the vain manner that it is. But He will have His own children to pray: "Hallowed be thy name." If we love God and know Him, we will want His name to be honored. We shall feel hurt if people invoke His name in vain. Our desire will grow stronger and we will pray more earnestly: "Hallowed be thy name." Till one day, all will hallow this name, and none will dare to take His name in vain.

"Hallowed be thy name." God's name is not just a title which we use with our mouth to address Him; it is a great revelation which we receive from the Lord. God's name in the Bible is used to signify His own revelation to men in order that they may know Him. His name reveals His nature and manifests His perfection. This is not anything that the human soul can understand, it requires the Lord himself to manifest it to us (see John 17.6). He says, "I made known unto them thy name, and will make it known; that the love wherewith thou lovedst me may be in them, and I in them" (John 17.26). To know God's name requires repeated revelations of the Lord.

"Hallowed be thy name." This not only is our heart desire but also constitutes our worship to the Father. We ought to give glory to God. We should commence our prayer with praise. Before we anticipate His mercy and grace, let us glorify God. Let Him receive the praise due His perfectness; and then shall we receive grace from Him. The preeminent and the ultimate of our prayer is that God may get glory.

"Hallowed by thy name." God's name is linked with His glory. "I had regard for my holy name, which the house of Israel had profaned among the nations, whither they went" (Ez. 36.21). The people of Israel had not hallowed God's name, they had instead profaned that name wherever they went. Yet God had regard for His holy name. Our Lord requires of us this holy desire. In other words, He wishes to glorify God's name through us. The name of God must first be hallowed in each individual heart, and then this our desire will be deepened. The cross must do a deeper work in us before we can glorify God's name. Otherwise we cannot view it as a holy desire but only a whimsical fancy. This being the case, what dealing and purification we need to receive in our lives!

The second desire is "Thy kingdom come". What

kind of a kingdom is this? Judging from the context, this has reference to the kingdom of the heavens. In teaching us to pray "Thy kingdom come", the Lord is saying that there is the kingdom of God in heaven, but that on this earth there is not, and that therefore we ought to pray to God to extend the boundary of the kingdom of the heavens to reach to this earth. The kingdom of God in the Bible is spoken of in geographical as well as in historical terms. History is a matter of time, whereas geography is a matter of space.

According to the Scriptures, the geographical factor of the kingdom of God exceeds its historical factor. "If I by the Spirit of God cast out demons," said the Lord Jesus, "then is the kingdom of God come upon you" (Matt. 12.28). Is this a historical problem? No, it is a geographical problem. Wherever the Son of God casts out demons by the Spirit of God, there is the kingdom of God. So during this period of time, the kingdom of God is more geographical than historical.

If our concept of the kingdom is always historical, we have then seen but one side of it, not the whole thing. In the Old Testament, the kingdom of the heavens is merely prophesied. With the coming of the Lord Jesus, John the Baptist first proclaims that the kingdom of the heavens is at hand; the same proclamation is made by the Lord Jesus himself later on. Why? Because here begins to appear the people of the kingdom of the heavens. And when we come to Matthew 13, the kingdom of the heavens even begins to have an outward appearance on earth. Today wherever the children of God cast out demons by the Spirit of God, and destroy their work, there is to be found the kingdom of God. The Lord teaches us to pray "Thy kingdom come" because He anticipates the kingdom of God filling the earth.

"Thy kingdom come"! This is not only a *desire* of the church, it is also a *responsibility* of the church. The church ought to bring the kingdom of God to earth. In order to accomplish this task the church must be willing to pay any price, submitting herself to the restraint and control of heaven that she may be the outlet of heaven, letting through the authority of heaven onto earth. If the church is to bring in the kingdom of God she must not be ignorant of the devices of Satan (see 2 Cor. 2.11) and she needs to be clothed with the whole armor of God that she may be able to stand against the wiles of the devil (Eph. 6.11). For upon wherever the kingdom of God comes down, the demons will be driven out of that place. When the kingdom of God rules over the earth completely, Satan will be cast into the bottomless pit (see Rev. 20.1–3).

Since the church has such enormous responsibility, it is no wonder Satan attacks her with all his power. May the church pray like the saints of old, saying, "Bow thy heavens, O Jehovah, and come down" (Ps. 144.5) and, "Oh that thou [God] wouldst rend the heavens, that thou wouldst come down" (Is. 64.1). May she say to Satan, "Depart from me . . .

into the eternal fire which is prepared for the devil and his angels" (Matt. 25.41).

The third desire is "Thy will be done, as in heaven, so on earth". This reveals that the will of God is done in heaven, but that on earth it is not wholly done. He is God; who can hinder His will from being done? Is it man who hinders God or is it Satan? Actually none can hinder Him. Then why such a prayer? In order to answer this question we need to be clear on the principle of prayer.

Throughout the entire Bible are to be found a number of basic principles of truth, among which is the principle of prayer. Now let us immediately recognize that the very fact that prayer is found in the Bible is most amazing. We learn in the Scriptures, do we not, that God knows beforehand what we need. Then why should we pray at all? For since God is omniscient, then according to human logic there is really no need for men to pray! Yet this is the amazing thing about the Bible; that it tells how God wants men to pray! Prayer is this: that God desires to do a certain thing, yet He will not do it alone; He waits until men on earth so pray, and only then will He do it. He has His own will and mind, nevertheless He waits for men to pray. Not that God does not know our need, but that He will supply our need only after we have prayed. He will not move till somebody prays.

The reason for us to pray, therefore, is because

God waits for men to pray before He will do anything. The Lord Jesus is to be born, but there needs to be Simeon and Anna praying (see Luke 2.25, 36–38). The Holy Spirit is to come, but the one hundred and twenty must pray for ten days (see Acts 1.15, 2.1–2). Such is the principle of prayer. Can we through prayer make God do what He does not want to do? Not at all. Nonetheless, He waits until we pray for that which He desires to do before He does it.

When Ahab was king, the word of the Lord came explicitly to Elijah, saying, "I will send rain upon the earth." Yet He did not pour down the rain till Elijah had prayed (see 1 Kings 18.1,41–45). God refuses to carry out His will alone; He wants us to pray before He executes His will. So what is prayer? It is as follows: first, God has a will; second, we touch His will, hence we pray; and third, as we pray, God hears our prayer.

How great is the mistaken concept that in praying to God man initiates the thing which man wants God to do. The Bible shows us that it is God who first has a will, it is God who desires to do a certain thing. He makes known His will to me that I may utter it. This is called prayer. Here the Lord Jesus teaches us to pray, for it is God himself who wishes to have His name hallowed, His Kingdom come, and His will to be done on earth. But God will not automatically bring these to pass; He waits for the church to pray. You pray, I pray, all the children of God pray. And when this prayer reaches the saturation point, God's name shall then be hallowed among men, His kingdom shall come, and His will shall be done on earth as in heaven.

God's children must learn this kind of prayer—that they must always be sensitive to what God wants to do. Though the will of God is already formed, He will nevertheless not perform it till His children's mind is stirred and they express His will through prayer. Then shall He begin to hear that prayer. Even if the moment awaits the millennium when His name is to be hallowed, His kingdom is to come, and His will is to be done on earth, this timing may be hastened or delayed according as to how God's children pray. And the basic reason for this is: that God refuses to do His will alone—He instead wants His children on earth to pray before He does it.

Many things may be deemed to be God's fragmentary wills, but God has a supreme will which includes all these fragmentary wills. As we are attentive to God's supreme will, all these fragments will eventually be fulfilled. God in heaven has His will; His Spirit communicates this will to us, causing us to cry with one accord, "O God, we want You to do this thing." Only then will God do it. This is what the Bible tells us concerning the principle of prayer.

The work of God today is affected by our prayer on earth. May we ask Him to open our eyes that we may see how the action of heaven is influenced by our prayer on earth. Our Lord has explained this mystery of God which was hidden through the ages. If we are willing to offer ourselves, spending time in prayer, we will soon realize that such prayer will not only be heard by God but will be rewarded in the future too.

God's will is like the water of a river, and our prayer is like a channel. If our prayer is big enough, the answer will likewise be big; if our prayer is limited, the answer too will be restricted. The Welsh Revival of 1903–04 may be considered to be the greatest revival in the history of the church. God used a miner Evan Roberts as a vessel for this great revival work. He did not possess much learning, but his prayer was exceedingly deep. Later on he withdrew from public work for seven or eight years. One day a brother met him and asked what he had been doing during those years. He answered in but one sentence: "I have been praying the prayer of the kingdom."

Brethren, do we realize that without prayer the kingdom will not come? If the channel is blocked, can the water flow out? Through the prayer which the Lord here teaches us the thought and demand of God are revealed. At the time when the will of God's children is wholly one with the will of God, the kingdom of God shall truly come and His will shall indeed be done on earth as it is in heaven.

Three Requests for Ourselves

In the second section of Jesus' teaching on prayer, we have three requests for ourselves.

We first of all read: "Give us this day our daily

bread." Some people have trouble in understanding
how the Lord can teach us to pray for God's name,
God's kingdom, and God's will, but then suddenly
turn to the matter of daily bread. The plunge in
prayer from such sublime heights to such a mundane
level seems like a sudden descent of ten thousand
feet. But let us recognize that there is a very good
reason for it.

The Lord takes note of the person who truly
belongs to God and prays constantly for the name,
kingdom, and will of God. Since such prayer is so
essential, the one who prays will invariably draw
down upon him the assault of Satan. There is
therefore one matter which needs to be prayed
for—daily bread. Food is man's immediate need; it is
a great temptation. When a person's daily bread
becomes a problem, this constitutes an exceedingly
great temptation. On the one hand, you desire that
God's name be hallowed and you pray that His
kingdom will come and His will be done on earth; on
the other hand, you as a person still live on earth and
have need of daily bread. Satan knows about this
necessity of yours. And hence you must exercise this
protective prayer. This is a Christian's prayer for
himself, asking the Lord for protection. Otherwise,
while he prays such transcendental prayer he will be
attacked by the enemy. Satan can assault us in this
area. If we are in need of daily bread and are
assaulted in this regard, our prayer will be affected.
May we see the necessity of this prayer. As long as we

are still on earth as human beings our bodies have this need of daily food. Consequently, we must ask God to give us our daily bread.

This prayer also shows us how we need to look to God daily and to pray to Him daily. For so the Lord teaches us here, saying, "Give us *this day* our daily bread." It is not praying weekly, but rather daily. We have nothing to lean upon on earth, nor do we have any savings. We have to request our daily bread for *today*—not for a week's or a month's supply. How we must rely on God! Here we see that our Lord is not unmindful of our daily bread, neither does He teach us not to ask, but He wants us to ask daily.

Now as a matter of fact our Father knows already the things which we need. Yet the Lord here wants us to pray to God every day for our daily bread because the Lord longs that we learn to look to the Father daily, thus exercising our faith from day to day. How often we become anxious for too far ahead and so we pray for remote needs. This we should not do. Let us realize that if we have a strong desire for God's name and kingdom and will, our trouble will automatically become great. But since God gives us *this day* our daily bread, we can pray for our tomorrow's bread when tomorrow comes. "Therefore do not be anxious about tomorrow, for tomorrow will be anxious for itself. Let the day's own trouble be sufficient for the day" (Matt. 6.34 RSV).

The second request is: "Forgive us our debts, as we also have forgiven our debtors." We have the request for physical need on the one hand and the request for a conscience without offense on the other. Day by day we cannot avoid offending God in many areas. Though these may not all be sins, they nonetheless can be debts. What should be done and has not been done is debt; what should be said and has not been said is also debt. Hence it is not very easy to maintain a conscience void of offense before God. Each night before retiring we discover that many things have happened during the day which are offensive to God. These may not necessarily be sins, nevertheless they are debts. As we ask God to forgive our debts and to remember them no more we are able to have a conscience without offense. This is extremely important. Having our debts as well as our sins forgiven, we now have a clear conscience to live with boldness before God.

Many brothers and sisters have the following kind of experience: that whenever there is offense in conscience, faith is unable to rise up. For conscience cannot afford any leak. As the apostle Paul has said: "Holding faith and a good conscience; which some having thrust from them made shipwreck concerning the faith" (1 Tim. 1.19). Conscience can be likened to a ship which cannot suffer any leak. If there is leak in conscience, faith is lost. Conscience cannot tolerate any debt or offense. Whenever there is a grievance a hole is created; and the first to leak out will be our faith. If there is a hole in conscience, and no matter how we may try, we just cannot believe. As soon as a condemning voice is raised in conscience, faith immediately leaks away. For this reason we must keep a conscience void of offense. We should ask God to forgive our debts. This is a most serious matter. And although this is not related to the problem of our having eternal life, it is definitely connected with the problem of our fellowship and God's discipline.

We ask God to forgive our debts as we also have forgiven our debtors. If a person is hard bargaining towards his brothers and sisters and cannot forget their offenses towards him, he is not qualified to ask God to forgive his debts. He whose heart is so narrow as to always notice how people have hurt and offended him is unable to pray such a prayer before God. We need to have a forgiving heart before we can come to the Father with boldness, asking Him to "forgive us our debts as we also have forgiven our debtors." We cannot ask God to forgive our debts if we have not also forgiven another's debts. How can we open our mouths to ask for God's forgiveness unless we have first forgiven our debtors?

Brethren, if you are dissatisfied with some people because they have not met your requests and if you are always calculating in your heart how much this one or that one has offended you, how can you ever pray this prayer to the Father? Since you must ask the Father to forgive whatever debt you owe Him, must you not likewise forgive the debts others owe you? You need first to forgive your debtors, and then you can pray to the Father with boldness: "Forgive me my debts as I also have forgiven my debtors."

Here may we notice this one thing, that besides telling us of our relationship with the Father, the Bible also shows us our relationship among brothers and sisters. A brother or a sister deceives himself or herself if he or she considers himself or herself as right with God because he or she remembers the relationship with God although neglecting the relationship with other brothers and sisters. If we have this day created a discord with any brother or sister, we instantly lose the blessing of God. Likewise too, we incur a debt—though not a sin—if we today fail to do or to say what we ought to our brothers and sisters. Let us not fancy that as long as there is not sin everything is fine; we must also not have any debt. If we can neither forgive nor forget whatever grievances we have against our brothers or sisters, this will hinder us from receiving God's forgiveness. Just as we treat brothers and sisters, so God will also treat us. It is a serious self-deception if we reckon God has forgiven our debts to Him while simultaneously we continue to remember our debtors, counting and complaining all the time. For the Lord explicitly teaches us to pray: "Forgive us our debts, as we also have forgiven our debtors."

Please notice the words "As . . . forgiven". Without "forgiven", how can there be "as"? If you have not forgiven your debtors, your debts will still be remembered by God. In case you *have* forgiven your debtors from your heart and have allowed these debts to pass completely away as though there were nothing, you can then come to God with boldness, saying, "Forgive me my debts as I also have forgiven my debtors." And the result is that God cannot but forgive your debts. Do let us happily fulfill "forgive our debtors", lest the lack thereof affect our own forgiveness before God.

And the third request? "Bring us not into temptation, but deliver us from the evil one." The first request pertains to our physical need; the second request is concerned with our relationship with brothers and sisters; this final one speaks of our relation with Satan. "Bring us not into temptation" is the negative side, whereas "deliver us from the evil one" is the positive. As we live on earth for God with a strong heart desire for His name, His kingdom, and His will, we on the one hand will have physical need for which we must look to God to supply our daily bread, and on the other hand will experience the need of a conscience to be ever clean and blameless before God and for which we must ask Him to forgive us our debts. Yet there is another need we encounter—the need to have peace, for the sake of which we ask God to deliver us from the hand of Satan.

Brothers and sisters, the more we walk in the way of the kingdom of the heavens, the stronger will be our temptations. How should we cope with the situation? We should pray, asking God: "Bring us not into temptation." Never be so self-confident as to dare to face any temptation. Since the Lord has taught us thus to pray, we ought to ask God not to lead us into temptation. We do not know when temptation will come, but we can pray beforehand that God will not bring us into it.

Such prayer is for the sake of protection. Instead of waiting daily for temptation to come upon us, we should daily pray that the Lord will not bring us into it. Only whatever is permitted by the Lord may come to us; but what He does not permit, we ask that it may not happen to us. Otherwise, we will be so occupied with fighting against temptation from dawn to dusk that we can do nothing else. We must ask the Lord to not lead us into temptation, so that we may neither meet those whom we should not meet nor encounter the things which should not happen to us. This is a kind of protective prayer. And we ought to pray to God for this protection, asking Him to give us our daily bread, to solve our problem of a clean conscience, and to not bring us into temptation.

We should not only ask the Lord: "Bring us not into temptation" but also: "Deliver us from the evil one." This latter side is a positive request. No matter where the hand of Satan is—whether it pertains to our daily bread or to his accusing our conscience or to whatever temptation with which he may tempt us—we ask the Lord to deliver us from the evil one. In other words, we do not expect to fall into the hand of the evil one in anything. By reading Matthew 8 and 9 we may realize that the hand of Satan is on more things than we assume. With respect to the human body, his hand may be in terms of a high fever; with respect to the sea, a sudden storm. His hand may show itself through demon possession in the case of man or through drowning in the case of a herd of swine. It may also be reflected in rejection of, or opposition to, the Lord in human hearts without cause. In any event, Satan is out to hurt people and to cause them to suffer. We should therefore pray, asking the Lord to deliver us from the evil one.

Our three heart desires for God form the basic prayer; our three requests for ourselves become protective prayer. Our prayer for daily bread is not merely for eating, neither is our request for a conscience without offense only for a good feeling, nor is our asking to be delivered from the evil one simply for the sake of not being harmed. What motivates our prayer is that we may live on earth and do more of the work of prayer—thus expecting the name of the Father to be hallowed, His kingdom to come, and His will to be done on earth as in heaven.

Three Praises

Finally, the Lord teaches us to praise God for three things: "For thine is the kingdom, and the power, and the glory, for ever. Amen." Such praises declare that the kingdom is the Father's, the power is the Father's, and the glory is the Father's. These three matters to be praised are related to the deliverance from the evil one; yea, even more so, they are related to the whole prayer which our Lord has taught. The reason for asking to be delivered from the evil one is because the kingdom is the Father's, not Satan's; because the power is the Father's, not Satan's; and because the glory is the Father's, not Satan's. The emphasis is right here: that since the kingdom is the Father's, we ought not fall into Satan's hand; and that since the power is the Father's, we must not fall into Satan's hand; and that again, since the glory is the Father's, we shall not fall into Satan's hand. This constitutes a very strong reason. If we fall into Satan's hand, how can the Father be glorified? But if it is the Father who rules, then Satan has no power over us. The kingdom of the heavens belongs to the Father, therefore we cannot and we should not fall into the hand of Satan.

Concerning power, we ought to remember the words our Lord has said to us: "Behold, I have given you authority to tread upon serpents and scorpions, and over all the power of the enemy; and nothing shall in any wise hurt you" (Luke 10.19). The authority which the Lord says He has given over-comes all the power of the enemy. For there is power in that authority. The Lord wishes us to know that in the kingdom there is an authority, and behind that authority is the power which is all-controlling. The kingdom is God's, not Satan's; naturally the author-ity is also God's, not Satan's; and the power too is God's, not Satan's. And as to glory, it likewise belongs to God and not to Satan. The kingdom and power and glory being all God's, those who belong to Him can expect to be delivered from temptation and from the hand of Satan.

In the New Testament the name of the Lord

usually represents authority, while the Holy Spirit represents power. All authority is in the name of the Lord; all power is in the Holy Spirit. The kingdom speaks of the rule of heaven, hence it is God's authority. The Holy Spirit is the power by which God acts. Since the kingdom is God's, Satan has nowhere to rule; since the power is the Holy Spirit, the adversary has no means by which to compete. We are told in Matthew 12.28 that as soon as the demons meet the Holy Spirit they are immediately cast out. And finally, the glory is also God's. Hence we may loudly declare and highly praise: "Thine is the kingdom, and the power, and the glory, for ever. Amen."

The Lord teaches us to pray after this manner. This is not to recite it as a formality, but rather to pray according to the principle revealed by this prayer. This should form the basis for all prayers. For the sake of God, we earnestly desire that His name be hallowed, His kingdom come, and His will be done on earth as in heaven. Likewise, too, for the sake of the fact that the kingdom and power and glory are God's, we give Him all the praises. Since the kingdom and power and glory are all His, God's name ought to be hallowed, His kingdom ought to come, and His will ought to be done on earth as in heaven. Since the kingdom and power and glory are His, we should pray to him for our daily bread, for the forgiveness of our debts, and for deliverance from temptation and the evil one. All our prayers should be modeled after this one.

Some people have insinuated that this prayer is not given to us Christians because it does not conclude with "in the name of the Lord". Such insinuation is plain folly. Because the prayer which the Lord teaches us here is not a form prayer. Moreover, we wonder which prayer in the New Testament ends with the words "in the name of the Lord". When, for instance, the disciples cried to the Lord in the boat, saying, "Save, Lord; we perish" (Matt. 8.25), were there such words as "in the name of the Lord" included? It is clear that the Lord is not teaching us to say the exact words; rather, He wants us to pray according to the principle He hereby gives. He enumerates the various elements we should pray for, without telling us to repeat these very words.

The Importance of Forgiving

Now once the Lord has concluded His teaching on prayer, He follows up immediately with: "For if ye forgive men their trespasses, your heavenly Father will also forgive you. But if ye forgive not men their trespasses, neither will your Father forgive your trespasses" (Matt. 6.14,15). It is here that the Lord explains to us the meaning of "Forgive us our debts, as we also have forgiven our debtors" (v.12).

How very easy it is for a Christian to fail in the matter of forgiving. If there be such an unforgiving spirit among God's children, then all that they have learned—together with all their faith and all their power—will appear to leak away. Hence the Lord speaks quite distinctly and quite emphatically here. They are very simple words, yet God's children need these simple words: "If ye forgive men their trespasses, your heavenly Father will also forgive you." It is so simple to obtain the forgiveness of the heavenly Father. But, "if ye forgive not men their trespasses, neither will your Father forgive your trespasses." There is no such thing as casual forgiveness. These words are simple, yet the things behind the words are not so simple. If we say with our lips that we forgive, yet in our heart we do not forgive, this cannot be reckoned in God's eyes as our having forgiven others' trespasses. Forgiving in lips but not in heart is empty word, a lie, and therefore not accredited before God. We must forgive from our heart. Just as the early disciples needed these words, so we need them today too.

If Christians regard others' trespasses and do not forgive from the heart, the church soon gets into trouble. Now of course if we do not live on earth as a church we may not need mutual forgiving, since we may each go our own way when we disagree. But the Lord knows how important is our relationship to one another. So He reiterates the point at the very end with emphasis. He knows that the more we have fellowship and communication with one another, the more we need to forgive. In order to impress us with its importance, He cannot but draw our attention to it. If we cannot forgive one another, we will easily give ground to the devil. If we do not forgive one another, we are not living in the kingdom nor are we doing the work of the kingdom. No one who fails to forgive men their trespasses is able to do the work of the kingdom; none who lacks this forgiveness is able to live in the kingdom. We need to remember that whenever we are at odds with brothers and sisters we are also in controversy with the Lord. We cannot pray on the one hand and be unforgiving on the other. Brethren, this is not an insignificant matter. We must notice what the Lord stresses here; we need to forgive men their trespasses.

Lastly, let us be aware of the attention the Lord gives to prayer. When He speaks of alms before He speaks of prayer, He uses only four verses; when He mentions fast following prayer, He uses merely three verses. But on prayer, He talks quite lengthily and emphatically. For prayer is directly related to God, and it is the most important factor in Christian work. He shows us that there is reward for such prayer because the prayer herein mentioned has tremendous consequences attaching to it. All who are faithful to this work of prayer shall be rewarded in the future. Whoever continues in this kind of labor in secret will not go unrewarded. May God raise up people to pray for the work of God.

And one final point. In this prayer which the Lord teaches, the pronoun "we" is used throughout. This is the tone of the church, this is prayer with body consciousness. It is an exceedingly great prayer. Who can reckon how many saints on earth have prayed this prayer? May we once again renew our consecration and join the ranks of those who pray this great prayer. May the Lord have mercy on us that we too may participate in this great prayer work.

3 In the Name of the Lord Jesus— The Trust of God

Scripture Reading: Phil. 2.9–11; John 14.13–14; 15.16; 16.23–24,26a; Mark 16.17; Luke 10.17–20; 24.47; Acts 3.6; 4.7,10,12; 10.43; 16.18; 19.5; 1 Cor. 6.11

One matter which we especially have to understand before God concerns the name of the Lord Jesus. No one on earth can be saved except by the name of the Lord Jesus; and none can be a useful vessel in God's hand unless he knows the name of the Lord Jesus. We must therefore understand what the name of the Lord Jesus means. How sorely to be lamented is the fact that the name of the Lord Jesus has become too common in human language! How frequently such phrases as "in the name of Jesus Christ" or "in the name of the Lord Jesus" become almost meaningless! People are so used to reading and hearing these words that they fail to comprehend their significance. Let us ask God to lead us back to the real meaning of the most familiar name of our Lord Jesus.

ONE

The name of the Lord Jesus is very special. It is something which Christ did not possess while on earth. When He was on earth His name was Jesus. This is what Matthew 1 tells us. But in Philippians 2 it is further indicated that the Lord having humbled himself unto death—even the death of the cross—God has also highly exalted Him and given Him a name which is above every name. What is this name? Let us read Philippians 2.10–11—"That in the name of Jesus every knee should bow, of things in heaven and things on earth and things under the earth, and that every tongue should confess that Jesus Christ is Lord, to the glory of God the Father." This name is "the name of Jesus". Was He not called Jesus while on earth? Yet this is a name given Him after He had ascended to heaven. Because of His obedience to God even unto death—and that the death of the cross—the Lord is exalted and given a name which is above every name. And that name above every name is the name of Jesus.

It is not only Paul who, having received revelation, says that the name of the Lord Jesus has undergone this great change; even the Lord Jesus himself shows us that His name has undergone a drastic change: "Hitherto have ye asked nothing in my name: ask, and ye shall receive, that your joy may be made full. . . . In that day ye shall ask in my name" (John 16.24,26a). "In that day", says Jesus, not today; but just wait until that day and then you shall ask in My name. On the day He spoke these words He had not yet had this name that is above all names. But He receives that name above all names "in that day", and "in that day" we can go to the Father and ask in His name.

May God open our eyes to see that after His ascension the name of the Lord Jesus has undergone a great change—a change which is beyond the comprehension of our mind. That name is a God-given name; that name is above all names.

TWO

What does that name represent? It represents authority as well as power. Why does it represent authority and power? "That in the name of Jesus every knee should bow, of things in heaven and things on earth and things under the earth, and that every tongue should confess that Jesus Christ is Lord, to the glory of God the Father"—this is authority. Whoever he is, he should bow in the name of Jesus; whoever he is, he should confess that Jesus is Lord. For this reason the name of Jesus means that God has given Him an authority and power which exceeds all.

On one occasion Jesus' disciples said to Him:

"Lord, even the demons are subject unto us in thy name" (Luke 10.17). It was a great thing to the disciples to be able to cast out demons in the Lord's name. The demons are not afraid of the many big names in this world, but in the name of the Lord Jesus they are made subject to the disciples. Later on the Lord Jesus explained to His disciples why the demons were subject to them in His name: "Behold, I have given you authority . . . over all the power of the enemy" (v.19). Hence the name is equal to authority.*

Even the rulers of the Jews were aware of this. For after Peter had caused the lame man to walk, the rulers questioned the apostles on the next day, asking them: "By what power, or in what name, have ye done this?" (Acts 4.7) In other words, what authority did you have in making this man to walk? They knew that to act in one's name was to be given an authority. Consequently, the name of Jesus stands for the authority which God has entrusted to Him. Not that the name is authority, but that the effect of the name is authority.

THREE

The New Testament not only shows us the name of Jesus, it also includes a most special phrase—

---

* The authority and power of the name of Jesus is here demonstrated in anticipation of the ascension of the Lord.— *Translator*

namely, "in the name of the Lord Jesus". Have we truly realized this? There is told us not simply the name of Jesus Christ but *in* the name of Jesus Christ is mentioned as well. If we study the word of God carefully and in the meantime we really seek to walk in the spiritual way, we cannot but acknowledge how many have been the times that we have said "in the name of the Lord Jesus" or "in the name of Jesus Christ" without actually knowing how to use that name. How can we be normal Christians if we do not even know how to use the name of the Lord Jesus? Let us therefore see what is indeed meant by "in the name of the Lord Jesus".

In the various conversations of the Lord Jesus, the first time we meet the words "in the name of the Lord Jesus" is in the Gospel of John. It is found in the conversation between our Lord and His disciples after He had washed their feet. In John Chapters 14, 15, and 16, He especially tells His disciples what they can do if they do it in His name—"And whatsoever ye shall ask in my name, that will I do. . . . If ye shall ask anything in my name, that will I do" (14.13,14). In Chapters 14 through 16 He is constantly saying to the disciples, "In my name". It indicates to us that not only will He one day receive from God a name which is above all names but that also His name is something which the disciples may use. A name which you as well as I can use. This name is given by God to His Son Jesus, and God's Son Jesus Christ in turn commits this name to your hand and mine that we all may use it. So that the Bible mentions not only the fact that the Lord Jesus has a name which is above all other names; it also tells us the experience of using the name of the Lord Jesus. There is not only His name but also in His name. The name of Jesus Christ is what He has received from God; in the name of Jesus Christ is what the children of God share in His name. Do we realize that this is the greatest trust God has entrusted to us?

Why is it that the name of Jesus is God's trust? What is a "trust"? God entrusts us to preach the gospel; He enjoins us to do a work; He charges us to go somewhere or utter a few words. All these are God's trusts. Yet the meaning of "in the name of the Lord Jesus" is a different kind of trust. It means God trusting you to do something; yea, but even more so, He is trusting you with His Son. It is not God sending you out, it is a taking of God's Son with you. Now this is what is meant by "in the name of the Lord Jesus".

"In the name of the Lord Jesus" actually signifies that God has entrusted His Son to us. Let us use an illustration. Suppose you deposit a sum of money in the bank. And suppose, further, that the withdrawal of any amount requires a certain seal of yours. One day you entrust a friend to withdraw some money from the bank and you give him your seal. It is rather simple for him to withdraw the money, since he has your seal in his hand. If he writes ten dollars on a blank check and stamps it with your seal he will obtain the ten dollars from the bank. In like manner, "in the name of the Lord Jesus" is similar to your having the Lord Jesus give you His seal. Let us suppose again that I have a large amount of money deposited in a bank and that I am ready to trust a person by my giving him my check book and seal. For were I not to trust him, how would I know but what he would fill in the blank checks and take away all my money? How would I know but what he would sign a contract with my seal? If I do not trust him, I would never put my seal into his hand in the first place. But if I in actual fact do give him my seal, it signifies that I am going to acknowledge whatever thing he does. And this is precisely what is meant by the term "in the name of the Lord Jesus"—which is, that the Lord Jesus dares to entrust His name to us and to let us use it. He trusts us to the degree that He dares to commit himself to us, and at the same time He is willing to accept the responsibility for whatever consequence or relationships we may involve Him in by using His name.

Sometimes we tell a person: "You go and tell a certain brother that he ought to do thus and so. If you are asked who says this, you can answer that I say so." This is what is meant by "in my name". It simply means using the name. You give your name to a certain person; he uses your name; and you are responsible for whatever he does in your name.

During His last night on earth with the disciples the Lord Jesus said to them: "Whatsoever ye shall ask in my name, that will I do, that the Father may be glorified in the Son" (John 14.13). He entrusted them with something of tremendous value; He gave

His name to them. His name is authority; there is nothing greater than what He has given us. Just imagine what will happen if we use the name which the Lord Jesus has committed to us adversely. Here, for example, is a man who holds great power. Each time he gives an order it becomes effective if he puts his seal on it. Suppose he gives his seal to another person. He will have to be responsible for whatever order this other man issues that has his seal attached to it. Do you think he will carelessly entrust his seal to just any person? Of course not. Yet the Lord Jesus has committed His name to us. The name of the Lord Jesus is above all names. He is nevertheless willing to entrust His name to us. Do we truly appreciate what responsibility He has taken upon himself in giving His name to us? And whatever we do in His name, that will God bear responsibility for. This is indeed tremendous! That whatever is done in the name of the Lord Jesus God will be responsible for!

FOUR

One special feature of today is that the Lord Jesus does not act directly. He does not speak directly to the world, He instead speaks through the church on earth. Neither does He work miracles directly, but performs them through the church. Nor does He save people directly; rather, He saves them by the church. Since the Lord Jesus does nothing today directly by himself but all is done through the church, therefore He entrusts His name to the church.

What a great responsibility He has taken upon himself! It is much easier to be responsible for the things one does oneself than to be held responsible for things done by others. If you hold your own seal, you are only answerable for the things you yourself do; but should you put your seal into another's hand, you will be held accountable for all that he does with your seal. If the Lord Jesus had remained in this world until today, His work would have continued to be done by himself as He once earlier did, and He would not have needed to be responsible for us. However, His current work is not done directly by His own self; He has instead entrusted His work to the church.

Today all work of the Lord Jesus is in the church. What the church does today is what the Lord Jesus does. And therefore the Lord Jesus is held accountable for all which the church does in His name. If we trust somebody to do a certain thing, we will rescind our trust immediately if ever he is proven to be untrustworthy. The Lord Jesus, however, must trust the church to the very end, because today the Son of God is no longer in the flesh but is in the Spirit and in the church. He cannot but trust the church, else He has no way of doing anything today. The Lord Jesus has indeed ascended to heaven, and is now seated at the right hand of the Father waiting for His enemies to become His footstool. He is there as the great high priest, making intercession for us. This is now His heavenly work. But as to His work on earth, that He has entrusted to the church. For this reason the church has the authority today to use His name, and the Lord Jesus will bear all responsibility for whatever the church does in His name.

The church cannot obtain a greater authority on earth than the authority vested in the name of the Lord Jesus. In giving His name to the church the Lord Jesus has granted the greatest trust. For this name represents His very own self. Saying anything in the name of the Lord Jesus becomes what the Lord Jesus himself says; doing anything in the name of the Lord Jesus becomes what the Lord himself does. Whatever is decided in His name is reckoned as decided by Him. The church has the authority to speak in the name of the Lord Jesus. What a trust God has given to the church!

Let us look at an instance in the Bible when the name of the Lord was invoked. When Michael the archangel contended with the devil over the body of Moses, he did not say "I rebuke you"; nor did he say "May the Lord rebuke you"; for if the word "may" had been injected it would have become a prayer or an expectation. No, Michael declared, "The Lord rebuke thee" (Jude 9). It clearly means that when I am rebuking you, it is the Lord himself who rebukes you. Michael the archangel used here the name of the Lord. So that in invoking the name of the Lord Jesus it is not necessary to utter the exact words.

Using the name of the Lord Jesus in the same way as we use our own name is what is meant by "in the name of the Lord Jesus". We are touching upon a most significant spiritual experience here when we say that we may today use the name of the Lord Jesus just as though we were using our own name. Many confess that they have not experienced fully the power of the blood of the Lord. We rejoice to profess the fact that we have not yet fully experienced the power of the name of the Lord. To the Corinthian believers Paul is able to say: "I have no command-ment of the Lord: but I give my judgment. . . . And I think that I also have the Spirit of God" (1 Cor. 7.25,40). We really need to be brought by God to such a point to be able to see that this name is a name which we can use.

Do we realize that here is a name which is both authority and power which is put into the hand of the church to be used? The church ought to use the name of the Lord wisely. We sometimes say that the church does rule, but how can she rule without having the name? She holds the keys of the kingdom and is responsible to bring in the kingdom; yet without this name she is unable to open up the kingdom. The purpose of God is indeed to swallow death by life in the church and to bind Satan through the church; but except we have this name and know how to use it, we will not be able to fulfill our mission. We must consequently see that this name is given by the Lord Jesus to the church.

FIVE

It is for this very reason that as soon as one believes in the Lord Jesus and is saved he is commanded by God to be baptized. What does baptism do for us? We are baptized into the name of the Lord Jesus: "When they heard this, they were baptized *into* the name of the Lord Jesus" (Acts 19.5). When I receive baptism I have a share in that name. Henceforth I am entrusted with that name. I can thereafter use the name of the Lord Jesus just as I use my own name. In view of this, baptism constitutes a tremendous thing. In spiritual reality, I am now a resurrected man. Because I stand on the ground of death and resurrection I may use the name of the Lord Jesus. From this day onward I am related to His name; He is Christ and I am a Christian. What are Christians? What is a church? None else than a group of people on earth who may use the name of the Lord Jesus and have God responsible for that name. However that name is used, God takes up the responsibility for whatever lies behind it. Is not this stupendous? Our relationship with the name of the Lord Jesus begins at baptism, for we are baptized into that name.

Here we see how imperative are the cross and resurrection. Only by standing on the ground of baptism can we use the name of the Lord Jesus; otherwise we are disqualified from using that name. If the cross is unable to get through in our life, the Lord

Jesus will not be effective in us. We will not be competent to use that name; but even should we use it, God will not back us up and assume responsibility. You and I must stand on the ground of baptism, which means we believe in the reality of the cross— acknowledging that our old man was crucified with Christ and accepting also the principle of the cross in dealing with our natural life. Baptism is an assurance: that all we are needs to go through death daily; only what little is left after going through death has any spiritual usefulness. What is destroyed upon passing through death cannot stand before God. For God wants only what remains after passing through the cross—that which death cannot destroy.

The children of God need to see the reality of the cross. We need to see through revelation of God what we have obtained in Christ. There must be a day when the backbone of one's natural life is broken by the Lord; then shall we be useful. This is not a doctrine; this is life. The day must come when God can see in your life and mine the marks of the cross. Many people do not seem to have the cross worked into their lives. Their words, their deeds, their feelings, and especially their attitudes before God bear no evidence of the cross. It is necessary that one day God break that man by the cross. Whatever is left after passing through the cross is called resurrection. For resurrection is whatever cannot be buried nor annihilated after going through death. Resurrection is what we have left to us upon our being stricken by the Lord. Those who stand on such ground as this are alone able to use the authority of the Lord Jesus, even the name of the Lord Jesus. And as they use this name, God will back them up and bear the full responsibility.

Now this is truly the highest trust in the whole wide world. God can entrust the name of His Son to you and me and allow us to use it as we would our own name. This really is exceedingly great. The responsibility which God undertakes in this respect is beyond comprehension.

SIX

When we use the name of the Lord Jesus what will be the effect of this name? From the Scriptures we can see effects in at least three areas—towards men, towards the devil, and towards God.

Manward Effect

"Repentance and remission of sins should be preached in his name unto all the nations, beginning from Jerusalem" (Luke 24.47). "To him bear all the prophets witness, that through his name every one that believeth on him shall receive remission of sins" (Acts 10.43). "And such were some of you: but ye were washed, but ye were sanctified, but ye were justified in the name of the Lord Jesus Christ, and in the Spirit of our God" (1 Cor. 6.11). Especially is this effect seen in the words of Acts 3: "And a certain man that was lame from his mother's womb was carried, whom they laid daily at the door of the temple which is called Beautiful, to ask alms of them that entered into the temple; who seeing Peter and John about to go into the temple, asked to receive an alms. And Peter, fastening his eyes upon him, with John, said, Look on us. And he gave heed unto them, expecting to receive something from them. But Peter said, Silver and gold have I none; but what I have, that give I thee. In the name of Jesus Christ of Nazareth, walk" (vv.2–6).

Brothers and sisters, do you know what it is to speak to people in the name of Jesus of Nazareth? How will you fare in such a situation if you have not been standing on the ground of death and resurrection, if you are not on the ground of baptism? If you are not on this ground, then you will probably kneel down and pray something like this: "Lord, I do not know if this lame man should be healed. If he should be healed, make it so clear that we may have the boldness to ask; if he is not to be healed, then we will leave him alone." But the experience of the apostles is not so. They do not consider the name of the Lord Jesus as remaining with the Lord Jesus; on the contrary, they take the name of Jesus of Nazareth as theirs, that which they possess and which they may use.

What is the church? The church is made up of people who keep the name of the Lord Jesus on earth. Those whom God has called out of the nations to be gathered together unto His name form the church. The church is to maintain on earth the name of the Lord Jesus; and consequently, she can use that name on people. Sometimes we are able to tell people: "Arise, and be baptized, and wash away thy sins, calling on his name" (Acts 22.16). While the Lord Jesus was on earth He once told a woman: "Daughter, thy faith hath made thee whole; go in peace" (Luke 8.48). On another occasion He said to a man with palsy: "Man, thy sins are forgiven thee" (Luke 5.20). If we stand on the ground of baptism and meanwhile we have vision and revelation, we will know that we are managers of the name of the Lord Jesus. As you and I preach the gospel to people and notice that they have received the gospel, we may say to them: "Brother, go in peace, for the Lord Jesus has forgiven you."

Because the lame man was healed, the rulers, the elders and the scribes had the apostles stand in their midst, and inquired: "By what power, or in what name, have ye done this?" To which Peter, filled with the Holy Spirit, replied: "Be it known unto you all, and to all the people of Israel, that in the name of Jesus Christ of Nazareth, whom ye crucified, whom God raised from the dead, even in him doth this man stand here before you whole. . . . And in none other is there salvation: for neither is there any other name under heaven, that is given among men, wherein we must be saved" (Acts 4.10,12). There is only this name, and none else, wherein we are saved. Hence we may use this name towards men.

Devil-ward Effect

We may not only use this name towards men but also use it towards the devil. "In my name shall they cast out demons" (Mark 16.17). How do we use the name of the Lord Jesus in casting out demons? It is recorded in Acts 16 that Paul once met a certain maid having a spirit of divination who troubled him for many days. What did Paul do when he was "sore troubled"? He did not go to pray; he instead turned and said to the spirit: "I charge thee in the name of Jesus Christ to come out of her" (v.18). By this charging in the name of Jesus Christ the spirit came out of her that very hour. Here we see how the name of the Lord Jesus was entrusted to the hand of Paul that he might use that name. Let us further observe that the name of the Lord Jesus is not committed to our hands to simply remain as a deposit in heaven. If our spiritual condition is normal His name is entrusted to our hands. So that when Paul was sore troubled, instead of praying to the Lord he simply charged the spirit in the name of the Lord to come out. We would think of such a man as being unspiritual, independent, and lacking in a seeking of God's will. We note, though, that when he cast out the spirit in the name of the Lord, the spirit was cast out. Therefore, the real question is a matter of how we live before God—whether or not we stand on the ground of death and resurrection. If we do, the Lord's name is in our hand. "In the name of the Lord

Jesus" is not an empty phrase. It is a name you and I may use to work and to cast out demons.

In Luke 10 the Lord is seen sending out His disciples. Though at that time He had not yet ascended to heaven, He nonetheless acted on ascension ground. So that He proclaimed: "I beheld Satan fallen as lightning from heaven" (v.18). When the disciples went out to work, the Lord Jesus did not go with them, but they took His name with them. They returned rejoicing, saying, "Lord, even the demons are subject unto us." Why was this true? Because "the demons are subject unto us *in thy name*" (v.17). With the name of the Lord in their hands they had authority with them. Hence the Lord Jesus subsequently declared: "Behold, I have given you authority to tread upon serpents and scorpions, and over all the power of the enemy" (v.19). Do we see, then, that we may use the name of the Lord Jesus to deal with all the power of the enemy? How we need to have our eyes opened to see that the name of the Lord Jesus which God has given to us is God's trust.

Godward Effect

One more area is to be seen here. Beside the fact that the name of the Lord Jesus enables us to cause people to be saved and to be healed as well as to have authority over the devil and to cast out demons, there is the especially precious effect of the name in that it makes possible for us to come to the Father and have our words heard. In John Chapters 14 through 16 the

Bible mentions things concerning the name of the Lord Jesus three times. Let us say this reverently that the Lord Jesus is most daring! What does He say here? "And whatsoever ye shall ask in my name, that will I do, that the Father may be glorified in the Son. If ye shall ask anything in my name, that will I do" (14.13–14). Oh, this name that is above all names! At this name every mouth in heaven, on earth, and under the earth shall confess that He is Lord, and every knee shall bow to Him! How powerful is this name before God. God respects this name, hence He will hear us when we ask in this name. Just listen to this: "Ye did not choose me," says the Lord Jesus, "but I chose you, and appointed you, that ye should go and bear fruit, and that your fruit should abide; that whatsoever ye shall ask of the Father in my name, he may give it you" (15.16). And again: "In that day, ye shall ask me no question. Verily, verily, I say unto you, If ye shall ask anything of the Father, he will give it you in my name. Hitherto have ye asked nothing in my name: ask, and ye shall receive, that your joy may be made full" (16.23–24). Brethren, just consider whether there be any promise greater than this one!

Let us clearly understand that what is meant by praying in the name of the Lord Jesus is that we are saying to God: "Oh God, I am undependable and useless, but I come in the name of the Lord Jesus." Suppose, through a messenger, you send a letter to a friend in which you ask him to deliver over to the bearer of the letter the money you had deposited with him. After your friend examines the signature and finds it to be right, will he not then hand the money over to the messenger? Of course he will. How absurd if he should call the messenger in and ask him questions such as, "Have you been to school? What is your family situation? How are your home folks? What is your temperament?" No, no. He does not care who the messenger is. All he cares about is whether or not the signature is his friend's. The messenger comes in the name of his friend, and his friend trusts this man. Hallelujah! When I stand before God in the name of the Lord Jesus, this is to say that I am not here on my own but in the name of the Lord; it is not because of what I have nor of what I will be, but simply because of the name of the Lord. The prayers of many people are only expected to be answered in the future. They hope that after they become better and better their prayers will be answered. Let us see, however, that the reason we can pray is due to His name, not to our own name. We stand before God in His name: because of Him, not because of ourselves; by His blood, not by our righteousness; according to His will, not according to ours.

To know the name of the Lord is a revelation, not a doctrine. There ought to be a day when God will open our eyes to see the power and the majesty of this name. How wonderful that God should commit this name to us. After God has given the name of His Son to us, we may say in return: "God, in the name of Your Son Jesus." This means: "God, You believe in me, You trust me; whatever I do, You hold Yourself responsible." With such a name in our hand to deal with men and the devil and God, what kind of a life must we live in order to have the power to use it! In view of this, we must daily learn to know the cross. Remember that the cross and this name are inseparable. May the cross work deeply enough in our lives so as to cause us to know how to use this name towards men and the devil and God. May God give the church abundant knowledge of this name that even now it may have its place restored, its authority and power recovered. May the church enjoy spiritual riches in the name of the Lord.

4 Authoritative Prayer

Scripture Reading: Matt. 18.18,19; Mark 11.23,24; Eph. 1.20–22; 2.6; 6.12,13,18,19a.

ONE

In the Bible can be found a kind of prayer which is the highest and the most spiritual, yet few people notice or offer up such utterance. What is it? It is "authoritative prayer". We know prayer of praise, prayer of thanksgiving, prayer of asking, and prayer of intercession, but we know very little of prayer of authority. Authoritative prayer is that which occupies a most significant place in the Word. It signifies authority, even the command of authority.

Now if we desire to be men and women of prayer, we must learn this authoritative kind. It is the

type of prayer which the Lord refers to in Matthew
18.18—"What things soever ye shall bind on earth
shall be bound in heaven; and what things soever ye
shall loose on earth shall be loosed in heaven." Here
is loosing as well as binding prayer. The movement of
heaven follows the movement of the earth. Heaven
listens to the words on earth and acts on the earth's
command. Whatsoever is bound on earth shall be
bound in heaven; and whatsoever is loosed on earth
shall be loosed in heaven. It is not an asking on earth
but a binding on earth; it is not an asking on earth
but a loosing on earth. And this is authoritative
prayer.

Such an expression can be found in Isaiah 45.11,
which runs: "Command ye me." How do we dare to
command God? Is not this too preposterous? too
presumptuous? But this is what God himself says.
Doubtless we should not in the least allow the flesh to
come in here. Nevertheless we are hereby shown that
there is a kind of commanding prayer. According to
God's viewpoint we may command Him. Such utterance needs to be learned specifically by all students
of prayer.

Let us review the story of Exodus 14. When
Moses led the children of Israel out of Egypt he came
to the shore of the Red Sea. A serious problem arose.
Before them was the Red Sea and behind them were
the pursuing Egyptians. At that moment the Israelites
were truly in a dilemma. They saw the Egyptians
coming after them, and they were sore afraid. They
cried to the Lord on the one hand and murmured

against Moses on the other. How did Moses react? From the word of God we learn that Moses cried to the Lord. But then God told him: "Wherefore criest thou unto me? speak unto the children of Israel, that they go forward. And lift thou up thy rod, and stretch out thy hand over the sea, and divide it; and the children of Israel shall go into the midst of the sea on dry ground" (vv.15–16). The rod which God gave to Moses represents authority. So that what God meant by His words was: You do not need to cry to Me, you may use authoritative prayer; you pray the prayer of command, and I will work. Hence what Moses learned and experienced here was authoritative prayer or the prayer of command.

TWO

In our day where does such prayer of command find its origin with the Christian? It has its origin at the ascension of the Lord. Ascension is very much related to the Christian life. What is the relationship? Ascension gives us victory. Just as the death of Christ solves our old creation in Adam, and resurrection leads us into the new creation, so ascension gives us a new position in the face of Satan. This is not a new position before God, for such position is obtained by the resurrection of the Lord. Nonetheless, our new position before Satan is secured through the ascension of Christ.

Note these words from Ephesians: "And made him [Christ] to sit at his right hand in the heavenly places, far above all rule, and authority, and power, and dominion, and every name that is named, not only in this world, but also in that which is to come: and he put all things in subjection under his feet" (1.20–22a). When Christ ascends to heaven He opens a way to heaven, so that henceforth His church may also ascend from earth to heaven. We know our spiritual foe dwells in the air; but today Christ is already ascended to heaven. A new way is therefore opened up from earth to heaven. This way was formerly blocked by Satan, but now Christ has opened it up. Christ is now far above all rule and authority and power and dominion and every name that is named, not only in this world, but also in that which is to come. This is the current position of Christ. In other words, God has caused Satan and all his subordinates to be subject to Christ; yea, He has put all things in subjection under His feet.

The significance of ascension is quite different from that of death and resurrection. While the latter is wholly for the sake of redemption, the former is for warfare—namely, to execute what His death and resurrection have accomplished. Ascension makes manifest a new position. Thank God, for we are told that He has "raised us up with him, and made us to sit with him in the heavenly places, in Christ Jesus" (Eph. 2.6).

Do we now see what God has done for us? In the first chapter of Ephesians we are told that Christ is ascended to heaven, far above all rule and authority and power and dominion and every name that is named, not only in this world, but also in that which is to come. In the second chapter it continues by telling us that we are now seated with Him in the heavenly places. This is the same as telling us that the *church* is also far above all rule and authority and power and dominion and every name that is named, not only in this world, but also in that which is to come. Thank God, this is a fact. As Christ is now in heaven far above all, so the church today too is far above all. As the Lord is far above all spiritual foes, so is the church far above all spiritual foes. As all spiritual foes are surpassed by the Lord at His ascension, so too are these spiritual foes surpassed by the church which has ascended with the Lord. Accordingly, all spiritual foes are put in subjection under the feet of the church.

Let us notice the connection between Ephesians 1, 2 and 6. Chapter 1 shows us our position in Christ; Chapter 2, the position of the church in Christ; and Chapter 6, what the church should do now that she has entered upon that position in Christ. Chapter 1 speaks of Christ in heaven; Chapter 2, of the church seated with Christ in the heavenly places; and Chapter 6, of spiritual warfare. God has made the church to sit with Christ in the heavenly places that she may not only sit there but also stand. So that when Chapter 2 mentions "sit", Chapter 6 says "stand", which signifies standing in the heavenly position: "Against the principalities, against the powers, against the world-rulers of this darkness, against the spiritual hosts of wickedness in the heavenly

places . . . and, having done all, to stand" (6.12,13).
Since our warfare is against the spiritual hosts of
wickedness, it is a spiritual warfare.

"With all prayer and supplication praying at all
seasons in the Spirit, and watching thereunto in all
perseverance and supplication for all the saints, and
on my behalf. . . ." (Eph. 6.18,19a). This is the
prayer of spiritual warfare. This kind of prayer is
different from the ordinary kind. The ordinary kind is
praying from earth to heaven, but the kind of prayer
here spoken of is a standing in the heavenly position
and praying from heaven down to earth. Authoritative prayer begins in heaven and ends on earth. In
short, authoritative prayer is a praying from heaven
to earth.

All who know how to pray know what is meant
by praying upward and what is meant by praying
downward. If a person has never learned how to pray
downward, he has yet to discover authoritative
prayer. In spiritual warfare this kind of praying
downward is exceedingly important. What is praying
downward? It is standing upon the heavenly position
Christ has given us and using authority to resist all
the works of Satan by commanding that whatever
God has commanded must be done. Suppose, for
example, that we are praying for a particular matter.
After we have seen what the will of God is and have
really ascertained what God has ordered, we should
then not pray: "O God, I ask You to do this thing";
on the contrary, we should pray: "God, You must do
this thing, it must be done in this way. God, this thing

must so be accomplished." This is commanding prayer—prayer of authority.

The meaning of "amen" is not "let it be so" but "thus shall it be". When I say amen to your prayer I am affirming that thus shall the matter be, that what you pray shall so be accomplished. This is the prayer of command, which comes out of faith. The reason we may so pray is because we have the heavenly position. We are brought into this heavenly position when Christ ascends to heaven. As Christ is in heaven so we too are in heaven, just as when Christ died and was resurrected, we also died and were resurrected. We ought to see the heavenly position of the church. Satan commences his work by causing us if he can to lose our heavenly position. For the heavenly is the position of victory. As long as we *stand* in that position, we are victorious. But if by Satan we are dragged down from heaven, we are defeated.

All victories are gained by standing in the heavenly, triumphant position. Satan will tempt you, saying, "You are on earth"; and you are defeated indeed if you answer, "I am on earth." He will use such defeat to trouble you, causing you to consider yourself as truly on earth. But if you stand and reply: "As Christ is in heaven, so I am in heaven", you lay hold of your heavenly position and are victorious. Hence standing in position is of great importance.

Authoritative prayer is based on this heavenly position. Because the church is with Christ in the heavenly places, she may pray the prayer of authority.

THREE

What is authoritative prayer? Simply explained, it is the type of prayer mentioned in Mark 11. In order to see the truth clearly let us read verses 23 and 24 carefully. Verse 24 begins with "therefore"—a connective term. So that the words in verse 24 are joined to those in verse 23. Since verse 24 speaks about prayer, verse 23 must also refer to prayer. What appears strange here is that in verse 23 it does not seem like an ordinary prayer. It does not say to God: "O God, please take up this mountain and cast it into the sea." What instead does it actually say? It reads there: "Whosoever shall say unto this mountain, Be thou taken up and cast into the sea."

What would the type of prayer be which is so often formed in our mind? We think in praying to God that it should always be: "O God, will You please take up this mountain and cast it into the sea?" But the Lord is talking about something quite different. He does not exhort us to speak to God, He instructs us to speak to the mountain. Not a speaking to God, but a speaking directly to the mountain— "Be thou taken up and cast into the sea." Lest we might not consider this as prayer, the Lord immediately explains in verse 24 that this is indeed prayer. Here is a word which is not directed to God, and yet it too is prayer. To speak to the mountain and command it to be cast into the sea is unquestionably a prayer. And this is authoritative in nature. For authoritative prayer is not asking God to do something but using God's authority to deal directly with problems, to get rid of all that needs to be got rid of. Such prayer needs to be learned by each and every overcomer. All who overcome must learn to speak to the mountain.

We have many weak spots such as temper, unclean thoughts, physical pains, and so forth. If we speak to God about them, we do not seem to be able to see quick corrections; but if we take the authority of God and speak to these mountains, we find them instantly removed. What is the significance of a "mountain"? Mountain represents the difficulty which stands in our way; it is that which blocks our path so that we cannot get through. When you and I meet a mountain, what will we do to it? Many when they encounter mountains in their lives or works will commence to pray, asking God to remove the mountain. Yet God tells us that we ourselves should speak to the mountain. It will be sufficient if we but command the mountain, declaring, "Be thou taken up and cast into the sea."

To ask God to remove the mountain and to command the mountain itself to move are two entirely opposite things. To come to God and ask Him to work is one thing, to directly command the mountain to move away is quite another thing. Such word of command is often neglected by us. It is very rare that we take the authority of God and speak directly to the difficulty, saying: "In the name of the Lord Jesus I ask you to leave me" or "I will not allow you to remain in my life." Authoritative prayer is for you to speak to whatever hinders you: "Depart from me." You will speak to your temper thusly: "Depart from me"; you will speak to your sickness as follows: "Depart from me, for by the resurrection life of the Lord I *will* get up." Not a speaking to God here, but a speaking directly to the mountain of hindrance, declaring: "Be thou taken up and cast into the sea." Now this is authoritative prayer.

What enables the church to have authoritative prayer? It is as the church has complete faith and doubts not that what she does is in perfect accord with God's will. Whenever we do not know the will of God we are unable to have faith. Consequently, before we do anything we need to first know whether it is God's will. If it is not God's will, how can we have faith? If we are in doubt as to God's heart, we shall also doubt the success of the undertaking.

Oftentimes we speak to the mountains casually; such speaking will not be effective since we do not even know God's will. But if we are clear before God as to what His desire is and doubt not, we may boldly address the mountain, saying, "Be thou taken up and cast into the sea", and it shall in fact be done. Here the Lord appoints us to be those who give command. We command what God has already commanded— and this is the prayer of authority.

Hence authoritative prayer is not asking God directly, it is applying God's authority directly upon the difficulty. We each have our mountain. It may not be the same size nor perhaps of the same kind. As a rule, though, whatever blocks you in your spiritual course is something you may command to depart from you. This is authoritative prayer.

Authoritative prayer is closely related to being overcomers. For Christians who do not know such prayer, they will not be overcomers. Let us ever be mindful that He who sits on the throne is God, He is our Lord Jesus Christ, and he who is in subjection to that throne is the enemy. Prayer alone can turn the power of God. Nothing can turn God's power to effect except prayer. Hence prayer is of utmost importance. If there is no prayer, how can we be overcomers?

Only those who know authoritative prayer know what prayer really is. The principal work of overcomers is to bring the authority of the heavenly throne down to earth. Today there is only one throne—God's throne; He alone rules and reigns far above all. To share in that authority, there must be prayer. How necessary is prayer. That which can move the throne can move anything and everything. We need to see that Christ has ascended to heaven far above all and that all things are put in subjection under His feet. Thus will we be able to use this throne-authority to govern all things. All of us must learn this authoritative prayer.

FOUR

How is authoritative prayer put into practice? Let us mention some small matters. For instance, suppose there is a brother who has done something wrong, and you feel you should go and admonish him. Yet one difficulty exists, and that is, you are afraid he may not listen to you. You are not sure whether he will accept your advice or not. However, if you know authoritative prayer, you may more easily manage this affair. You may pray: "Lord, I cannot go to him, but You ask him to come." You go to the throne to mobilize that brother. Sure enough, after a short while he comes to you and informs you personally, saying: "Brother, there is something I am not clear about; will you please tell me about it?" Thus are you able to admonish him most conveniently. This is authoritative prayer. Not doing anything in your strength, but doing it via the throne. Authoritative prayer is not begging God against His will, it is notifying Him of what you know must be done and He will do it.

Authoritative prayer may control weather as well as people. George Muller had such an experience. Once he was voyaging towards Quebec and encountered heavy fog. He talked to the captain of the ship: "Captain, I come to tell you that I need to be in Quebec City Saturday afternoon." "It is impossible," he replied. "Then if your ship cannot bring me there on time, God has some other way," said Muller. Whereupon he knelt down and prayed a most simple prayer. Then he said to the captain: "Captain, open your cabin door, and you will see that the fog has lifted." And when the captain got up to look he found that the fog had indeed vanished. Brother

Muller arrived at Quebec City Saturday afternoon and kept his appointment. This is authoritative prayer.

If God is to have a company of overcomers there must needs be prayer warfare. We need to battle with Satan not only when we encounter something but also when things happen around us. We must control them through the throne. No one can be an overcomer without being a prayer warrior. For one to be truly an overcomer before God he must learn to pray the prayer of authority.

The church is able to control hell by using authoritative prayer. Since Christ is far above all and the head of the church, the church is well able to control evil spirits and all who belong to Satan. How could she ever exist on earth if she were not given the authority to control evil spirits—if the Lord has not given such authority to her? She lives because she has the authority over all Satanic forces. Those who are spiritual know we may use authoritative prayer against evil spirits. We may cast out demons in the name of the Lord; we may contain the secret activities of the evil spirits by prayer.

The wiles of Satan are manifold: his evil spirits not only possess people in the open, he also works secretly in many ways. At times he works in the mind of man, therein injecting many evil thoughts such as suspicion, terror, disbelief, disappointment, imagination, or distortion so as to deceive and upset. At other times he steals away man's words and creates a certain thought which he presses into another person's mind that he may succeed in dividing and disturbing. We must use prayer to overcome all the various activities of the evil spirits. In meetings, at prayers, or in conversations we may first declare: "Lord, drive away all evil spirits and forbid them to have any activity in this place."

It is a fact that all the evil spirits are put in subjection under the feet of the church. If the church uses authority to pray, even the evil spirits will be subject to her. Authoritative prayer is not like any ordinary asking; it is the exercising of authority to command. Authoritative utterance is the prayer of command, saying, "Lord, I am willing", "Lord, I am not willing", "Lord, I will", "Lord, I will not", "Lord, I am determined to hear this", "Lord, I will not let this pass", or "Lord, only Your will be done, I want nothing else". When we use this authority, our prayer will achieve its goal. If there were more people in the church learning to pray in this manner, many more problems in the church would be easily solved. We should rule and manage the affairs of the church through prayer.

We must see that Christ has already ascended to heaven; otherwise, we have no power to direct. Christ is now the head of all things, and all things are put in subjection under His feet. He is the head over all things to the church. He becomes the head of all things for the sake of the church. And as Christ is head over all things to the church, all things must necessarily be under the church. This is what we need to take spiritual note of.

FIVE

Authoritative prayer may be divided into two sides: one side is the binding, the other side is the loosing. What things soever are bound on earth shall also be bound in heaven; and what things soever are loosed on earth shall also be loosed in heaven. What is done on earth shall also be done in heaven. This is Matthew 18.18. Verse 19 continues with prayer. So that the loosing as well as the binding are done through prayer. Loosing prayer and binding prayer are both authoritative prayers. Ordinary prayer will be asking *God* to bind and loose, but authoritative prayer is using authority to bind and loose by us. God so binds because the church has already bound; God so looses because the church has already loosed. God has given authority to the church; He will do whatever the church by that authority says.

Let us first discuss binding prayer. Many people and many things need to be bound. A brother is too talkative. He needs to be bound. You may go to God and pray: "O God, do not allow this brother to talk so much. Bind him that he may not do so." Thus will *you* bind him, but also *God* will bind him in heaven, so that he becomes less talkative. Or people may interrupt your prayer or your study of the Bible. Such people may be your wife or your husband, your children or your friends. You may use authority to utter binding prayer concerning these people who frequently interrupt you. You may say to God; "O God, bind them that they may not do anything to interrupt."

In a meeting some brother may say things which ought not to be said, may quote improper Scriptures, or may choose inappropriate hymns. Such a person needs to be bound. You may say: "Lord, So-and-so often errs; do not allow him to do these things any more." By so binding, you will see that God shall also bind him up. Sometimes some people will disturb the peace of the meeting—perhaps by talking, or crying, or walking to and fro. Such activities often occur in a meeting. And those who disturb are usually the same few people. These individuals and their acts need naturally to be bound. Therefore you say: "God, we notice that these people always disturb the meeting. Bind them and do not allow them to disturb." You shall see that if there are two or three on earth binding, God will also bind in heaven.

Not only all these disturbances need to be bound, but many of the works of the demons must be bound too. Each time the gospel is preached or testimony is given, the devil will be at work in human minds, whispering many words to them and injecting many ugly thoughts into them. Here the church must bind these evil spirits, forbidding them to whisper and to work. You should declare: "Lord, bind all the works of the evil spirits." If you on earth bind them, they shall likewise be bound in heaven.

The other side of authoritative prayer is loosing

prayer. What needs to be loosed? Let us illustrate this concretely. Many timid brothers dare not open their mouths in the meeting. They are afraid of witnessing, or of seeing people. We must ask God to release such brothers from the bondage that is upon them. Sometimes we may perhaps exhort them with a few words; but at many other times we need not say anything to them; instead we approach the throne for its control over the situation. There are people who really should come out and serve the Lord, nonetheless they are bound either by occupation, or affairs of family, or unbelieving mates, or outward circumstance. They may be bound by all kinds of bondages. But we can ask the Lord to loose them that they may step out to witness for the Lord. Brethren, are we aware of the need of authoritative prayer? Do we really see its urgency?

As to the matter of money, it too should be loosed through our prayer. Satan often tightens the pocket of man. Sometimes we should ask God to release the money that His work may not suffer due to financial lack.

Truth also needs to be released. We should frequently pray: "O Lord, release your truth." Many truths are so bound that they are not proclaimed; many truths are proclaimed but few hear and understand. For this reason, we should ask God to release His truth that it may get through to His children. In many places, truth seems to be barred from entrance; there appears to be no possibility for people to receive it. How we must ask God to release the truth that many churches under bondage may be released and many places which are closed may be opened up. The Lord alone knows how to send the truth to closed places. As we pray with authority, the Lord shall send in the truth. Let us therefore be alert to the many things which must be loosed through authoritative prayer.

We should pay special attention to binding prayer and loosing prayer. Many things need to be bound, many things must be loosed. Here we do not beg; rather, we use authority to bind and to loose. May God be gracious to us that we all may learn how to use authority in prayer. Not only must we learn how to pray, we must also know what is the victory of Christ. In the victory of Christ we release, in the victory of Christ we bind. We will bind all the things that are contrary to God's will. Authoritative prayer is heaven's rule on earth or the using of heaven's authority on earth.

Today we are but sojourners on the earth; in reality each of us is a heavenly person, therefore we have heavenly authority. Hence every one who is called by the name of the Lord is, on earth, a representative of the Lord. We are God's ambassadors. We have His life and have been delivered out of the power of darkness and been translated into the kingdom of the Son of God's love; consequently, we possess heavenly authority. At all times and in all places we hold the authority of heaven. We may control earthly affairs by means of heaven. May God give us grace that we may truly be prayer warriors for the Lord's sake, exercising His authority as over-comers that the victory of Christ may be manifested.

SIX

Finally, a serious warning is in order here; which is, that we must ourselves be subject to the authority of God. Except we are in subjection to God's authority we cannot exercise authoritative prayer. We should be subject not only to God's authority positionally but also in our daily life and practices; otherwise we will not have authoritative prayer.

Once there was a young man who went forth to cast out demons from a young woman. The demon suggested to the woman to take off her dress. Immediately the young brother exercised authority to command the demon: "In the name of the Lord Jesus I command you, I forbid you to remove the dress." "All right," replied the demon instantly, "if you do not permit me to take off the dress, I will not remove it." Now if the hidden life of that brother had been a failure, he would have been defeated before the demon; for the demon would not only have not obeyed that brother's command but he would also have exposed his sin.

We know that the creation was originally placed under the control of man. Why, then, does the creation not listen to man's command today? Be-cause man himself has failed to listen to God's word.

Why did the lion slay the man of God? Because he had been disobedient to God's command (see 1 Kings 13.20–25). But on the other hand, why did the lions not hurt Daniel when he was condemned to the lions' den? Because he was innocent before God and had done no hurt to the king. So God sent His angel to shut the lions' mouths (Daniel 6.22). So too, a viper could not harm the hand of Paul the servant of God (Acts 28.3–6), yet worms ate up the proud Herod (Acts 12.23). If we are subject to the authority of God we will be feared by the demons who also will be in subjection to our authority.

The Bible, moreover, reveals a close relationship between prayer, fasting, and authority. Prayer bespeaks our desire for God; while fasting illustrates our self-denial. The first privilege God granted to man was food. God gave Adam food before giving him anything else. So that fasting signifies a denial of man's first legal right. Many Christians fast without actually denying self; and thus their fast is not accepted as being such. The Pharisees fasted on the one hand but extorted on the other. If they had really fasted, they would have repaid what they had extorted. Since prayer is a desiring after God and fasting is a denying of self, faith will instantly be sparked when these two factors are joined. And then with faith, there is authority to cast out demons. Now if we desire after God yet refuse to deny self, we will not have faith and so neither will we have authority. But if we have both a desire for God and a denial of self, we shall instantly possess both faith and authority. We may quickly generate the prayer of faith, even unto authoritative prayer. And keep in mind that authoritative prayer is the most spiritual as well as the most important of prayers.

5 Watch and Pray

With all prayer and supplication praying at all seasons in the Spirit, and watching thereunto in all perseverance and supplication for all the saints. (Eph. 6.18)

The fragment of this verse upon which our attention will be focused is "watching thereunto in all perseverance". What does the word "thereunto" point towards? By reading the preceding clause we realize that it points at prayer and supplication. What the apostle means to say is that "with all prayer and supplication praying at all seasons in the Spirit" is still not enough, but that "watching . . . in all perseverance" must be added to prayer and supplication. In other words, there needs to be prayer on the one side and a watching on the other. What does "watching" mean? It means not slumbering; it means supervising or looking with eyes open; it means preventing any danger or emergency. Watching in prayer and supplication bespeaks having spiritual insight to discern the wiles of Satan and to discover the latter's end and means. Let us now enter concretely into some of the aspects of watching in supplication and prayer.

ONE

Prayer is a kind of service. It ought to be placed in a preeminent position. Satan always maneuvers to put other things concerning the Lord before prayer and to place prayer at the very last. However much people are reminded of the importance of prayer, not many really appreciate it. People are usually enthusiastic in attending meetings for ministry, Bible study, and so forth. They will find time for such meetings. But when it comes to prayer meeting, the attendance is so surprisingly minimal. No matter how many messages are given to remind us that our principal service is prayer and that if we fail in our prayer life we fail in everything, prayer is still not esteemed and is treated as a matter of little consequence. Faced with a pile of problems, we may say with our lips that only prayer can solve them, yet we talk more than pray, worry more than pray, and scheme more than pray. In sum, everything is put before prayer; other things are placed in prominent positions while prayer is relegated to last place; it is the only thing which is not so important.

One who knows the Lord deeply once said, "We all have committed the sin of neglecting prayer; we should tell ourselves: You are that man." We should say to ourselves indeed: You are the man! We should not blame others for not praying; we ourselves need to repent. How we need the Lord to enlighten our eyes that we may comprehend afresh the importance of prayer and know anew its value. Furthermore, we must recognize that had Satan not deceived us, we would not be neglecting prayer so much. We should therefore watch and discover therein all the various wiles of Satan. We will not allow him to delude us any more in relaxing in prayer.

TWO

After we are awakened to the importance of prayer and have offered ourselves to serve somewhat in prayer and to do a little of its work, we will be attacked incessantly by Satan so that we simply cannot find any time to pray. As we are just about to pray, someone will be knocking at the front door, or somebody else will come in through the back door. Either the grown-ups will quarrel or the children will disturb. If it is not a sudden sickness, it may be some unexpected happening. Before we decide to give ourselves to prayer, everything seems to be quiet; but the moment we wish to pray, all things break forth. Many unexpected and unforeseen events suddenly come upon us like ambushes. Numerous difficulties arise to hinder our prayer. They try to squeeze it out.

Are these coincidences? Most certainly not. They are not coincidental at all; they are Satan's planned strategy to hinder us from praying.

Satan is willing to encourage us to do many things if only he can succeed in squeezing out our prayer time. He well knows that spiritual work which is not established on the foundation of prayer has not much value and will eventually fail. Hence his strategy is to keep us so busy about other things that we neglect prayer. We are busily engaged from sunrise to sunset in work, in visitation, in hospitality, in preaching, so that prayer is pressed into a corner with little time left to pray.

Let us quote the words of a brother who knew the Lord deeply.

> When the children of Israel commenced to plan for their exodus from Egypt, the reaction of Pharaoh was to double their labor; Pharaoh's aim was to make them so much more occupied with work that they had no time to think of leaving Egypt. When you begin to plan or decide to practice a more abundant prayer life, Satan will start a new stratagem of making you busier, piling on your works, occupying your time with such needs that you have no opportunity to pray. I judge, dear brethren, that we must deal with this problem squarely. Naturally, in striving for a time to pray, there will be arguments concerning our mission, duty, and responsibility. Some people will consider such devotion to prayer as neglecting our mission, forsaking our duty, and impairing our responsibility. If we are confronted

with such a situation, we should bring our problems concerning mission, duty, and responsibility to the Lord and pray about them. (This kind of prayer may not be applicable to every believer, for it can be misunderstood. Some people will very much prefer to abandon their duty; they do not take up their responsibility seriously; they are far too eager to pass on their family affairs to others, professing that they will thus have time to pray. May the Lord protect these words from being misunderstood.) Let us recognize this point: That the enemy will use matters such as duty, mission, and responsibility to create his best arguments for stopping our prayer. Should we realize that our prayer life has been completely destroyed or that we have fallen into a restricted position in which we have no way to live a spiritual, ascendant and victorious life, we ought to say to the Lord: "O Lord, while I am praying, I commit my duty to You, and ask You to keep it from suffering any damage. I ask You to protect for me this time of prayer and forbid Satan to intrude, for I am using this time to seek Your glory." Here in the realm of prayer the principle of tithe may also be practiced. After you have offered to God His rightful portion, you will discover that by having offered one tenth to God, you can more efficiently use the nine-tenths that remain than even the entire ten tenths which you had before tithing. This principle of tithe is very effective.

Here must we realize this kind of prayer warfare. We should be strong and powerful, standing firmly on the ground of being in Christ and praying by the victory of the cross. We should utilize the complete victory of

Christ on the cross in striving for prayer, casting out the enemy from our prayer position so that we may keep it. This is likened to Shammah, a mighty man of David, who stood in the midst of a plot of ground full of lentils, and defended it, and slew the Philistines. The Lord worked a great victory through him (see 2 Sam. 23.11,12). This plot of ground full of lentils may represent our prayer position which needs to be guarded in the victory of Calvary from enemy intrusion. This is the kind of warfare for obtaining prayer, for the sake of prayer. I am quite concerned that we frequently accept circumstantial arrangement as an argument for thinking that prayer is currently impossible. Since things have been so aroused and have developed to such a point, we reckon it is now futile to speak of praying. Thus we give ground to the devil and are restricted by these things from prayer. Notice that this is a stratagem of the devil. In the name of the Lord and by His victory on the cross, we must sweep away all these obstacles to prayer. The cross is most effectual in gaining for us the time of prayer as it is always effective in other areas. Only, may we know how to exercise its victorious power.*

The above words provide us with much warning and exhortation. Brethren, we must fight for the prayer time, we must have time to pray. If we wait until we have some leisure moments to pray, we will never have the chance to pray. We should set apart

---

* Since the original quotation could not be found, this portion has been freely translated from the Chinese.—*Translator*

some definite time for prayer. "Those who have no set time for prayer," warns Andrew Murray, "do not pray." For this reason, we need to watch that we may get time to pray. We must also use prayer to protect this prayer time from being snatched away through the wiles of the devil.

THREE

We must not only be watchful in keeping the time of prayer but also be watchful during the prayer time so that we may really pray. For Satan will use his tricks to hinder our prayer while we are actually on our knees, just as he has previously made use of outward situations and all sorts of things to oppress us and thus keep us from having any time to pray in the first place.

Our mind is clear and our thought is concentrated; but as soon as we kneel down to pray our thoughts commence to be scattered: what should not be recalled is recalled, what should not be premeditated is premeditated, and many unnecessary notions suddenly dart in. All these thoughts were absent before prayer; but they now crowd in to disturb us just at the time of prayer.

Outside environment remains fairly calm, nothing really appears to be upsetting; but as soon as we kneel down to pray our ears seem to hear voices—actually the bleating of sheep and the lowing of oxen do not come from outside, yet strangely many voices arise to interfere with our prayer. Or we may be physically well, but as soon as we start to pray we become physically exhausted as though unable to continue. This is not due to any lack of sleep, for before praying we felt no weariness at all.

Sometimes strange symptoms that were not present earlier suddenly appear at the time of prayer. Prayer is originally meant to discharge burden; nonetheless as we kneel there to pray, not a word can be uttered and we feel as though we are suffocating. Many are the subjects of prayer, but at the moment of prayer we become paralyzed, cold, and lost. Even if we do manage to pray, it is like speaking to the air—completely fading out in two or three words.

All these above-mentioned conditions happen abruptly during the time of prayer. If we are ignorant of the devices of Satan in destroying our prayer, we will think of arising and giving up prayer. For the sake of prayer—for the sake of praying through—for the sake of discharging burden, we need to watch in prayer: watching against all and sundry conditions which hinder us to pray.

A battle is involved here. Before we pray we should first use prayer to ask God to enable us to pray; and during the time of prayer we should ask God to help us pray single-mindedly that our prayer will not be obstructed by any device of the enemy. We will speak to those disturbing thoughts, voices, weaknesses, and sicknesses: I oppose all these causeless phenomena as lies, as Satanic counterfeits. We will utter our voice to drive them away, we will not give any ground to the enemy. We must watch and resist the wiles of Satan with prayer that we may not only pray but pray through as well.

To pray through and to pray with strength is not a vain expectation. Ease and comfort will not get us into this prayer life, neither will we ever drift into this prayer life. We must learn a little, break a little, and fight a little to obtain such prayer.

FOUR

During prayer we must in addition guard against all that are not real prayers. We should know that Satan will not only prevent us from having time and power to pray, he will also cause us to waste the prayer time by our uttering many scattered, unrelated, unimportant, empty words as well as numerous vain requests. Our prayer time is so fully occupied with these things that our prayer is equal to zero. Many carnal, stale, long, routine, heartless, and ignorant prayers are simply a waste of time. These may sound like our own habitual prayers, yet the suggestion, instigation, and deception of Satan are not totally absent. If we are not watching, our prayer will become devoid of any meaning and consequence.

One brother cited the following story: "I read the record of Evan Roberts. Once several were in his home praying for a certain matter. In the middle of the prayer of one brother, Evan Roberts went over and put his hand over the mouth of the brother who was praying, and said, 'Brother, you do not need to pray on, for you are not praying at all.' As I read this incident I thought, How could Evan Roberts take such action? Yet he did take this action. And now I know that what he did was right." Many words in our prayer are spoken in the flesh by the instigation of Satan; they make the prayer quite lengthy but much is unreal and useless.

Is this not true? Often in praying, we seem to circle around the world. Time is spent and strength is exhausted, yet not a word of prayer strikes the mark. How can we expect such prayer to be heard by God? It has no spiritual value at all. Consequently, we must watch in prayer. Do not lengthen the time, do not give too many reasons; simply pour out your sincere desire before God and never use many vain words.

Let us be watchful lest we speak carelessly. One who knew how to pray wrote a poem in which was a sentence on prayer: "If you go before God to pray, prepare first what you want to ask." Brothers and sisters, if you do not even know what you want when you kneel down to pray, how can you expect God to hear your prayer? If your prayer is aimless and heartless, it is equivalent to no prayer. You fall into the trap of Satan, who makes you think you have prayed though actually you have not prayed at all. We need to be watchful so that each time we approach God we know beforehand what our heart desire is.

Do not pray without any desire in your heart. All prayers should be governed by heart desire. Look how our Lord pays attention to this. Bartimaeus, a blind beggar, cried out to the Lord: "Jesus, thou son of David, have mercy on me." The Lord Jesus answered him: "What wilt thou that I should do unto thee?" (Mark 10.47,51) Now the Lord will ask you precisely the same question: "What wilt thou that I should do unto thee?" Can you answer that question? Some brothers and sisters, after they have prayed for ten or twenty minutes, may not be able to tell you what they have asked God. Though many words are said in their prayer, nevertheless what is asked is even unknown to themselves. Such utterance is heartless and aimless, such cannot be considered as prayer. We must watchfully guard against any kind of prayer like that.

During prayer, words which can express desire are as important as the desire itself. Frequently there is a definite desire in our heart, yet after saying many words we seem to be farther away from the subject. This too needs to be watched. For the wile of Satan is either pulling you back from prayer or pushing you further out in prayer so that you become totally lost. How we must gird ourselves—not permitting the words of prayer to drift away from the subject, and drawing them back to the center if they do wander off. Always be on the alert to travel towards the goal, to disallow any unwanted words from mixing in, and to keep ourselves from praying prayers that are not prayers at all.

FIVE

Let us watch and pray. Never allow Satan to interrupt our prayer with his artifice. Satan frequently accuses us when we have suffered a little defeat. He will cause us to analyze ourselves while we are praying so that we seem hardly able to open our mouth before God. He will so discourage us when God's promise appears to be distantly vague that we lose the courage to wait on God further. Yet if our prayer is according to God's will, we should persevere in prayer. Even though we have failure, we can still come to God through the blood of the Lamb; there is no reason to let Satan interfere. We ought to be like that widow who came to the unrighteous judge so often that he avenged her (see Luke 18.5). We should be like the Shunammite who refused to leave until Elisha arose and followed her (see 2 Kings 4.30). We believe any delay in answer to prayer enables us to know something which we never knew before and to learn what we had never learned before. In any case, we will not permit Satan to cut off and destroy our prayer.

When a few of us are praying together Satan is not pleased. He will lay in our path all kinds of snares and make all sorts of moves to stop this prayer. Things such as groundless rumor, untrue story, causeless suspicion, growing misunderstanding, strange fear, and unfounded terror are secretly bestirred by Satan to create division, to shake the prayer meeting, and to destroy the oneness in prayer. In view of such Satanic attempts, we must "prove all things" (1 Thess. 5.21). Do not quickly believe, easily be moved by, or speedily spread any report. If we are watchful we shall discover that many of these unnecessary and inaccurate words and deeds are but the artifices of Satan whose aim is to weaken the heart and hand of God's people even to the splitting of them apart. Hence we must pray on the one hand and watch on the other. Let us follow the example of Nehemiah who set up watchers (Neh. 4.9). Our answer to Satan's threatening is: "There are no such things done as thou sayest, but thou feignest them out of thine own heart . . . Should such a man as I flee? and who is there, that, being such as I, would go into the temple to save his life? I will not go in" (Neh. 6.8,11). We shall not be frightened, neither shall we cease to pray. Once a brother said: "How much we need to set up watches to guard against the wiles of Satan, whose ways of destroying the corporate life of God's people far exceed our ability to count or list." In view of all this, we must watch in all perseverance and carefully inspect all things lest we give Satan opportunity to divide us, destroy our oneness in prayer, or cut off our prayer.

SIX

We must watch in our prayer lest it become vague. It is evident that many matters need to be settled, many people require intercession, the central message of God must be revealed, and not a few problems wait to be solved; yet at the time of prayer, there does not seem to be any definite subject for which to pray, and there is a total lack of words to express our prayer. We struggle to say two or three sentences before we cease altogether. Clearly Satanic assault is involved here.

No doubt on some occasions our prayer sounds routine because we are slothful, unconcerned, lacking in love, neither seeing nor being thorough; but at other times we really gather to pray and find our prayers feeble and few. This proves that something is interfering, and that very something is none other than Satan's plan to obstruct our prayer. Had we been watchful, we would have discovered that much of our forgetfulness, failure to recall, and tendency to drag are not attributable to us but are the effects of Satanic deceit, stealing, and robbing. We must oppose these guiles of Satan. Whether we pray for people or things, whether for truth or problems, we should pray out everything thoroughly. Bear in mind that a hasty prayer, a too economical prayer time-wise is usually a negligent prayer, which affords an easy loophole to the enemy. Let us not be lazy; instead let us on the one hand ask the Lord to enable us to recall all prayer burdens and to give us words to express these burdens; but let us on the other hand deal with our laziness and procrastination.

Our Lord rose up "in the morning, a great while before day . . . and there prayed." When Simon and his companions said to Him, "All are seeking thee",

His reply was, "Let us go elsewhere . . . that I may preach there also; for to this end came I forth" (Mark 1.35–38). How concrete and how thorough He is! Our Lord "went out into the mountain to pray; and he continued all night in prayer to God. And when it was day, he called his disciples; and he chose from them twelve, whom also he named apostles" (Luke 6.12–13). Once again, how concrete and how thorough! The apostle Paul reminded the saints in Ephesus to pray at all seasons in the Spirit, watching in all perseverance "and supplication for all the saints, and on my behalf, that utterance may be given unto me in opening my mouth, to make known with boldness the mystery of the gospel . . . that in it I may speak boldly, as I ought to speak" (Eph. 6.18–20). Such supplication is most concrete, distinct, and needy. If we have body consciousness and are really concerned about souls, saints, and the services of God's servants, we will have so many people and things for which to pray.

And as to each and every truth, there is also the need for much prayer. In writing to the saints in Ephesus Paul said, "For this cause I bow my knees unto the Father . . . that he would grant you. . . ." (3.14–19). From this we know that the revelation of the glorious truth which Paul received came from prayer, and prayer is the revelation. The real value of the light of truth comes by prayer. We should pray the truth into our life and then pray it out. We should pray much over the truths which we have heard and spoken so that these truths are not only remembered in our minds and written in our notebooks but will be manifested in our lives as well.

All these need concrete and thorough prayer! Behind various difficulties are demons who actually hold the rein. If we are not watchful we may consider these to be purely human or physical difficulties. But if we have spiritual insight we will see through these hindrances and so cast out the demons who hide behind them. Sometimes, as the Lord has indicated, "this kind goeth not out save by prayer and fasting" (Matt. 17.21 margin). This requires our watching on the one side and praying persistently on the other. Otherwise these difficulties will loom up like a mountain which forces you to travel around it instead of casting it into the sea. Oh that we may be awake, that we may pray thoroughly, expose all the wiles of Satan, destroy all his strongholds, and cast out all the demons behind every difficulty.

SEVEN

We must be watchful not merely before and during prayer but after it as well. We need to watch carefully all the changes which follow our prayer. All earnest prayers with burden are offered "with all prayers" and "at all seasons"—not only once but many times, not just in one direction but in all directions. So that after each prayer we should notice if there be any new discovery, any new change, any new movement.

It is not unlike Elijah's prayer at the top of

Carmel. He bowed himself down upon the earth and put his face between his knees. Seven times he sent his servant to go up and look at the sea till the servant reported that he saw a cloud rising out of the sea as small as a man's hand. Then he sent his servant to Ahab, telling the king to make ready the chariot and get down lest the rain stopped him (see 1 Kings 18.42–44). It is also not unlike Elisha praying for the child of the Shunammite. "He stretched himself upon him; and the flesh of the child waxed warm. Then he returned, and walked in the house once to and fro; and went up, and stretched himself upon him: and the child sneezed seven times, and the child opened his eyes" (2 Kings 4.34–36). Then he gave the child back to the mother. Neither Elijah nor Elisha simply knelt there to pray. Both of them prayed and then observed the effects of their supplications in changing environments.

Suppose you pray for one who opposes the Lord, asking God to make him believe. You pray for him with all prayers, and you also receive God's promise. Nevertheless, the outward situation seems to grow worse; he opposes the Lord more strongly than ever. You cannot disregard the change by continuing with your old prayer. You should notice it and tell it to God. If you are watchful you will receive light from God and know that your prayer has already influenced the unbelieving friend. You may begin to praise God. You should change your prayer and rearrange your net. Perhaps after a while his attitude turns soft and gentle. Once again you may change your prayer and set up a different net. Changing the prayer by observing the situation requires constant watchfulness.

Ephesians 6 is a chapter on spiritual warfare, the most important of which is the last mentioned prayer. Let us remember that the easiest target of attack in the life of a child of God is prayer. Therefore, we must watchfully press for the time of prayer, protect the prayer that is being prayed, prevent all that are not real prayers, and preclude Satan from interrupting our prayer with his evil devices. Know at all times that prayer is a ministry, a more excellent service. We should watch and pray, learn diligently to pray, and never allow Satan to have the smallest chance to destroy our prayer.